BEING AT HOME
IN THE UNIVERSE

BEING AT HOME IN THE UNIVERSE

Building an Internal Space

Richard Bellingham

iUniverse, Inc.
Bloomington

Being at Home in the Universe
Building an Internal Space

iUniverse books may be ordered through booksellers or by contacting:

iUniverse
1663 Liberty Drive
Bloomington, IN 47403
www.iuniverse.com
1-800-Authors (1-800-288-4677)

ISBN: 978-1-4759-8035-6 (sc)
ISBN: 978-1-4759-8036-3 (ebk)

Printed in the United States of America

iUniverse rev. date: 03/26/2013

CONTENTS

To Annie and Ezra who gave me a deeper appreciation of wonder and terror.

FOREWORD

One year ago I received an unexpected email from one of my 'original' students. He told me that he had been practicing daily the qigong I had taught him fifteen years ago and now he wanted to come to China to study with me. I was very proud of him since it is hard nowadays to find someone who can stick to something more than one workshop. Rick Bellingham was a man of action and he showed up at my doorstep in March, 2012.

I am very thankful for Dr. Bellingham, who not only 'paid' me a visit, but also taught me a lot about organizational skills. As you read his wonderful journey in China, please keep in mind that I am not a guru who possesses something that you don't have. Every one of us is already a spiritual being by birthright. My job is only to remind you who you are by channeling, if you will, the wisdom of 2,600 year old Lao Tzu and 2,400 year old Chuang tzu.

Human nature has not changed much over the thousands of years, as Steve Jobs put it: "We're born, we live for a brief instant, and we die. It's been happening for a long time. Technology is not changing it much—if at all." It is good news that human nature does not change over time. So we can still use the time proven method to train our body, mind and spirit for better results. Here is a secret champion training method written 2,400 ago in a Chuantze-tze Dasheng Chapter:

Once upon a time, there was a king who was fond of the game of cock fighting. One day the king received a big cock as a present, so he asked a Tao master to train it to fight. Ten days later, the king went to the training ground and saw his bird was big and strong. He asked the master "Is the cock ready to fight?" The master replied, "Not yet. Its body is strong and hard. It needs to soften up outside and remain strong inside."

Another ten days passed, the king went to the training ground again and saw his bird was flexible and alert. He asked the master "Is the cock ready to fight now?" The master replied, "Not yet. It's too eager to fight. It still reacts to sound and sight. It needs to learn to calm its mind."

Another ten days passed, the king went to the training ground again and saw his bird was calm and confident. He asked the master, "I am sure the cock is ready to fight now. Isn't it?" The master replied, "Not yet. It's too proud. It will be defeated by the humble ones. It needs to hide its Shen, the spirit inside."

Finally, after another ten days, the master brought the cock to see the king. The king was surprised to see the cock was standing there in stillness as if it were a wooden cock. "It is ready," the master proclaimed.

Immediately the king put the cock in the fighting ring. As soon as other cocks saw this special wooden cock, they all ran away in fear. So without a fight, the wooden cock became the true champion.

The training of the wooden cock is a process of simplification. It is like peeling the onion, layer by layer until it reaches simplicity, or the empty center. Sometimes we refer to this center inside our body as the Dantien, home of unconditional love. When one reaches home, the empty center, one simply becomes one with the universe. This means that when one focuses his whole being on a certain task, one will tap into the invisible power of Tao. Steve Jobs said: "That's been one of my mantras—focus and simplicity. Simple can be harder than complex: You have to work hard to get your thinking clean to make it simple. But it's worth it in the end because once you get there, you can move mountains."

For those who have realized Tao, being at home is not only feeling loved, secured, balanced, and joy but also feeling the invisible power of Tao, and the compassion for all living creatures.

Albert Einstein said: "A human being is a part of a whole, called by us the Universe, a part limited in time and space. He experiences himself, his thoughts and feelings as something separated from the rest—a kind of optical illusion of his consciousness. This illusion is kind of prison for us, restricting us to our personal desires and to affection for a few persons nearest us. Our task must be to free ourselves from this prison by widening our circle of compassion to embrace all living creatures and the whole of nature in its beauty."

No doubt Einstein is at home now. The difference between him and most of us is that he knew he was at home while he was alive. So where did we come from? Where are we going? The answer is simple: We are Tao, we have never left home.

Richard Bellingham

In this book, Rick distills the wisdom of three millennia, plus learnings from his own disciplined and rigorous journey, into a simple guide for spiritual growth. He travelled the world, both literally and figuratively, in search of truths that would help him develop a deeper and more meaningful understanding of life. What he discovered on his journey, and has shared with us in this book, in that this long and arduous effort leads to a short and effortless way home. You are already there.

So welcome home, I love you.

Master Luke Chan
March, 2013

PROLOGUE

By way of introduction, I was born and raised in a small, homogeneous, Midwestern town. I graduated from a local, public university in 1967—the peak of the Vietnam draft. My view of the world at that time was extremely narrow and provincial. In order to avoid being drafted, I enlisted in military intelligence with an assurance that I would spend my first year in German Language School and the remainder of my three year commitment in Germany. Six months later, I was in Vietnam.

My experience in Vietnam was the impetus for several transformations in my life. In short, my first 20 years were physically driven, the next 20 years were intellectually driven, the third 20 years were emotionally driven, and the last 10 years have been spiritually driven. Over the last 50 years, I have made great effort to figure out how we keep getting into unnecessary wars, both publicly and privately, and how we might find a different way. This book summarizes what I have learned on this rather unusual path.

My original intention was to share what I have learned about spiritual growth in general as well as some specific examples of my personal journey. The reason for wanting to share my learning and my journey is that I have come to believe ever more strongly that we are not only on a destructive course with terrifying consequences, but also that we are missing out on amazing possibilities as we limp mindlessly to oblivion. I don't pretend to be a religious scholar, an academic elite, or an enlightened guru. I have simply read a lot, worked hard on my development, and have had the good fortune of working with many brilliant people. I have sought whatever truth I could find from Eastern, spiritual mystics and have learned multiple processing constructs from Western social scientists. As I approach 70, I thought it might be helpful to future generations to learn a bit about some of my discoveries. Who knows, they may put the ideas to good use.

After spending several years working on *Being at Home in the Universe*, however, Eben Alexander published his book, *The Proof of Heaven*. Dr. Alexander is a Harvard neurosurgeon who went into a coma resulting from bacterial meningitis that caused his neo cortex to completely shut down. In *The Proof of Heaven*, Dr. Alexander shares the transcendental journey he had during his near death experience (NDE) while his brain was essentially dead. He also shares his transformation from a scientist who believes that consciousness only exists when the brain is functioning, to a scientist who believes that consciousness exists independent of the brain, and when the brain dies, it's "lights up." He tells his story of a whole new life after death in which he felt completely at One with the Universe—a life that was full of light, warmth, and love beyond imagination. Read his book for the whole story.

Dr. Alexander spent his entire career studying neuroscience and, after this phenomenal journey, applied his newly regained brainpower to the study of near death experiences. Meanwhile, for the last 40 years, I have been studying esoteric psychology and spiritual transformation in an attempt to tap into the light, warmth, and love that is available to us while we are still on earth. Thus, when *The Proof of Heaven* came out, I was thrilled that someone with such credibility would describe the experiences after death that could be approximated while we are still alive. I found it amazing that Dr. Alexander's description of his experiences, while considerably more intense, used exactly the same language that seekers of truth use in this life to pursue the eternal moment. Just as Dr. Alexander's NDE transformed his life, his book transformed the intention of this book to one dedicated to helping people prepare for death while we are still alive by increasing consciousness of the terror of our situation and gratitude for the wonder of our possibilities, i.e. to transform our lives from a mindless drill to a mindful dance while we are still alive.

Just prior to reading The *Proof of Heaven*, I had read *Incognito* and *Consciousness*—two books that reinforced what Dr. Alexander believed before his NDE, i.e. when the brain dies, consciousness dies with it—there is no soul that goes to a different place. And, modern neuroscience supports this belief that consciousness dies with the brain. As a behavioral scientist, I wanted to remain objective and accept the findings and breakthrough discoveries of preeminent neuroscientists, but I found it difficult to let go of my beliefs that 1) we can develop a soul on earth, 2) we can reach transcendental states of Oneness, and 3) there is a Nameless Source and Force that operates in the world. Reading *Proof of Heaven* inspired me to continue with renewed energy the work I had begun in this book. As a result of his book, I created the term "Near Life Experiences," which means that, even though we don't even come close to living as fully as we can in every moment, we have the opportunity to approach a fullness that approximates the experience Dr. Alexander had after his NDE. Only we can do it while we are still living. And we will prepare ourselves to navigate the transition between life, as we know it now, and the experience after death, which we can never know until we die, even though *The Proof of Heaven* hints at the possibilities.

Surely, many people will read Dr. Alexander's story as validation of their particular religious beliefs. There will be many clever bulletins announcing sermons such as "The Proof is in the Piety," or "Immortality Guaranteed." Ironically, religious doctrine and dogma can be detours on the journey that Dr. Alexander describes. *The Proof of Heaven* is about spiritual transformation, not religious indoctrination. Alas, I tip my hand. I am an irreligious person who has tried to forge a spiritual path independent of any institutional creed. It's not that I think that all religions are false. I believe there are many layers of truth and possibility in most religions. What I have tried to do, though, is find an internal HOME that is connected to higher forces, not an external refuge that institutionalized religions have tended to create and market. My intention is to simply describe what I learned on my path not to disparage other paths.

INTRODUCTION

At my older daughter's wedding, she sang the song, "Feels Like Home to Me" to her husband. It struck me that we are all searching for a sense of home in our lives and I was so grateful that she had found a man with whom she felt at home. Her beautiful voice filled the reception hall and my hope for everyone there was that they felt, in that moment, that they were home.

After several years of reflection on what HOME really means, I came to the conclusion that we search for HOME in all the wrong places. Some of us refer to the country we live in to be our home. "I can't wait to get home after travelling in all these foreign countries where I don't know the customs, I don't speak the language, and I don't like the food." Others identify the church or religion to which they are affiliated as their home. "When I enter the Temple, I feel at home." "When I go to the Mosque, I have a sense of peace." "When I go to Mass, I feel I belong."

How much of our problems stem from our need to find a home outside of ourselves—a sense of place where we feel like we belong and are loved—instead of looking inward and connecting to forces outward? This is the central question of this book. Some of the dictionary definitions for home are revealing:

1. a house, apartment, or other shelter that is the usual residence of a person, family, or household
2. the place in which one's domestic affections are centered
3. a dwelling place or retreat
4. the place or region where something is native or most common
5. of, pertaining to, or connected with one's home or country; domestic
6. principal or main
7. reaching the mark aimed at
8. deep, to the heart
9. into the position desired
10. toward its vessel
11. in a situation familiar to one; at ease
12. having safely achieved one's goal

The definitions above demonstrate the range of feelings that the word "home" elicits. For me, the first half of the definitions refer to external places (e.g. house, region, country) and resonate less than the words that speak to a returning, that describe a subjective and internal experience, and that lead to a feeling of peace and stillness. Picking and choosing from the list of dictionary definitions, one might define HOME as "reaching the mark arrived at deep in the heart, which enables a person to feel familiar, safe, and at one."

This book will explore ideas from esoteric literature and share some of my personal journey to find that HOME. It will describe the ideal end state, our current state, a process for closing the gap, and what it means to be "all the way back HOME where I belong."

This excerpt by Rebecca Ashton highlights some of the essential questions surrounding what it means to find a spiritual home.

> *"Nothing prepared me for the overwhelming feeling I had when I stepped off the plane in Cairo. A sense of relief ran through my body. I was back where I belonged. I was safe again. I thought this strange, though, seeing as I had never stepped foot in Egypt before.*

> *Why did this foreign land feel like home? It was 1994, a few years since I finished school. I had always loved my ancient history lessons so I was thrilled to be seeing the pyramids and Sphinx up close. But this feeling was something else.*

> *The rocks under my bare feet feel as familiar as an old friend; the air I breathe, warm and calming; the silence is my teacher. Since then, the Middle East has been a magnet to me. Is it the air? Is it the light? The color of the earth perhaps? Morocco, Tunisia, Libya, Syria, Qatar, and Jordan all followed. This is a place that feels like my own personal, spiritual precinct. I belong here. But not just a feeling of belonging to this land. This land is me and I it. A place I can never leave for too long because leaving it feels like leaving my spirit, a stealing of the heart.*

> *Lying against the earth at night, a sky full of infinite stars the last thing I see before drifting off to sleep. Being completely in tune with the cycle that is night and day. This is what I feel when I'm in my spiritual home. A lifting of the*

veil between here and the other side—the discovery of the internal god that is in us all. Sitting in stillness with that part of us we so often neglect.

But why is it mountains for some people, oceans for another, and why is it usually a very specific place? Maybe a little of each is true. But those who have experienced the emotional explosion of finding their spiritual belonging know of its importance.

Some of us have homes. And some of us have a spiritual home. A place where the soul soars, a deep and calm presence is surrendered to, and fear no longer exists. Some of us are blessed to return. Have you found your spiritual home?

I understand the appeal of different types of home. The house in which we were raised gives us a certain sense of home. It's where we return to after a day with friends, in school, or wherever we may go. Life partners can also bring a sense of peace and happiness and create a home of love and bonding. The hometown where we grew up grounds us in memories and gives us a sense of place. The home team for sports enthusiasts engenders a sense of loyalty, support, and rowdy displays of favoritism. The country in which we live and work gives us a sense of patriotism and obligation to serve in the defense of the homeland. The church to which people belong comforts them in hard times and challenges them to reach out and help others in good times. The core religious principles of faith, hope, and charity serve as bedrock principles for billions of people on earth. These are all good things. Our multiple homes give us a sense of security, pride, and belonging. It would be wrong to diminish the importance and purpose of these homes.

Indeed, I've been the beneficiary of several great homes. My parents were honest, decent, supportive, loving, and accepting people who always provided good food, comfortable space, and a few bucks for spending money now and then. I grew up in Plainwell, Michigan, a town that provided a solid education, winning sports teams, and a safe environment. I was raised as a Methodist and went to church with my family every Sunday. It seemed like a reasonable religious home for me at the time. Even though I didn't believe in the war, I still served my country in Vietnam and am supportive of protecting our homeland. America provided me with opportunities I could only have received in a few places in the world. It deserves my respect and patriotism.

The problem comes when we over-identify with any one of these homes. If we over-identify with our nationality, our religion, our profession, our job, or even as a sports fan etc., it starts a vicious cycle. Identification leads to imagination (feelings of superiority or being more than what we are), which leads to negative emotion (when others don't share your beliefs, patriotism, home team fanaticism, etc.), which leads to bitterness, hatred, and violence. It's not difficult to find the end-points of this cycle.

Religions and nations have been very effective at marketing the idea of providing a home for people. Nietzsche would say that religions manipulate the masses for purposes of power and control. Others would say that religions reach out to what's best in people. Ironically, in my view, churches have been more constructive on a sociological and psychological level than they have been on a spiritual level.

Nations have also conducted effective marketing campaigns based on the idea of protecting the homeland. Again, patriotism provides some positive benefits. It encourages loyalty, commitment and dedication and gives people a sense of place. On the other hand, it is a seductive way to manipulate young people into sacrificing their lives and engaging in violence for very dubious purposes. All we need to do is look at the death and destruction in Vietnam, Iraq, and Afghanistan to make this point.

It's strange that the debate around a sense of "HOME" can be so contentious. In *Proof of Heaven*, Dr. Alexander shares his encounter with a bright, white light in a near death experience and claims that this experience occurred after his brain had shut down in a coma. Other noted scientists claim that our brain is our only home and there is no soul or spirit outside it.

In the book *Incognito: The Secret Lives of the Brain*, neuroscientist David Eagleman describes consciousness as "a tiny stowaway on a transatlantic steamship, taking credit for the journey without acknowledging the massive engineering underfoot." He goes on to explain that we have multiple operating systems handling the details of ordinary life, which are largely inaccessible to our conscious minds and running primarily on auto-pilot. The degree to which an internal CEO emerges, who can observe how these operating systems are working, is a measure of our consciousness. As consciousness develops, we have some choice about the decisions we make in life, but only in limited amounts. We love to credit our consciousness for all the great decisions we make, but for the most part it sits on the sidelines as our brain cranks along according to historical evolution and cultural conditioning.

In the book *Consciousness*, Christof Koch, an MIT professor and research colleague of the DNA guru, Francis Crick, shares his confessions as a romantic reductionist. He reviews the ancient mind-body problem and shares the wellsprings of his inner conflict between reason and religion. He reinforces Eagleman's view that we are largely unaware of most of the things going on in our heads and that "zombie agents" control most of our lives, even though we confidently believe that we are in charge. Koch shares how saddened he was by the loss of his religious beliefs because it felt like losing the comfort of his childhood home, but how inescapable it was seeing the world as it is through a scientific lens. In a poignant closing to his book, Koch says that when all is said and done, he is left with an abiding sense of wonder. He closes his book with a psalm:

> *"So walk I on uplands unbounded*
> *And know that there is hope*
> *For that which thou didst mold out of dust*
> *To have consort with things eternal."*

These two books point out the most recent scientific discoveries about the extent to which we are able to increase our consciousness. Being at HOME in the universe requires high level consciousness and self awareness. Over the course of my career and spiritual journey, I have learned that consciousness and awareness can be increased dramatically but not without intentional effort. Being able to observe how our physical, emotional, and intellectual "zombies" operate is a critical first step to increasing consciousness. The extent to which these operating systems interact, particularly at higher levels, determines the state of our consciousness and our soul—the foundation for our HOME.

THE DESIRED END STATE

In his poem "The Guest House," Rumi encourages us to be grateful for whatever comes. Perhaps that's the best way to visualize the desired end state for our subjective, internal HOME.

This being human is a guest house. Every morning a new arrival.

A joy, a depression, a meanness, some momentary awareness comes as an unexpected visitor.

Welcome and entertain them all! Even if they are a crowd of sorrows, who violently sweep your house empty of its furniture, still, treat each guest honorably. He may be clearing you out for some new delight.

The dark thought, the shame, the malice. meet them at the door laughing and invite them in.

Be grateful for whatever comes. because each has been sent as a guide from beyond.

—Jelaluddin Rumi, tr. Coleman Barks

My aspiration for an internal HOME is to reach a state of being in which I am fully awake, unified, and conscious, even for fleeting moments. HOME is an acronym that describes that state:

I AM

> **H**ere
> at **O**ne
> In the **M**oment
>   **E**ternally

"I AM" means the focus is on being vs. doing. When kids graduate from high school or college, I prefer to ask them, "Who are you going to be?" instead of "What are you going to do?" In *The Way of Life*, Lao Tzu says that the way to doing is being. Being can best be described as a state of calmness, equanimity, peace and stillness that manifests as our Presence and defines our Essence.

"Here" means being fully present. Not distracted by physical preoccupations. Not lost in emotional disappointments. Not thinking about some intellectual challenge or new idea. It means being where you are.

"At One" means seeing ourselves as an integral part of the whole. Connected to the Universe. Connected to each other. Understanding that all is one and one is all. Not focusing on differences. Appreciating commonalities. Having a visceral sense of peace.

"In the Moment" means being here now. Not fretting about what happened in the past. Not worrying about what might happen in the future. Not tweeting, texting, e-mailing, reading. Focused. Centered.

"Eternally" means forever. Time and space no longer matter. We are experiencing a perfect moment that extends throughout eternity. It is a sense of immortality.

HOME is not discussed in terms of square feet, number of bathrooms, lot size, military might, economic power, athletic prowess, religious righteousness, or grandeur of any kind. As such, there is no need for greed, envy, or feelings of superiority. It's simple. Ironically, building this HOME is much more difficult than building nations, palaces, or churches.

THE CURRENT STATE

In short, the current state is that we are fighting the wrong wars in our life. We are more focused on the petty than the possible.

We can assess our current state by observing how much time we spend reacting to petty issues outside ourselves and how much time we spend pursuing what's possible inside ourselves. Essentially, that assessment lets us know how we are doing on our spiritual growth. Are we making real efforts to grow or are we coasting through life with half-hearted attempts to increase our consciousness and to build our internal HOME?

Instead of fighting wars about whose side some external God is on, this book suggests that the real war is confronting the challenges required to construct a virtual HOME within ourselves in entirely unconventional ways. We need to ask, "Are we fighting the right war or not?" Are we fighting with others about who is right, or are we fighting with ourselves to wake up and build our inner HOME?

This chapter overviews some of the internal challenges we need to confront and provides a radically different view of what is required to build our internal HOMES.

The construction plans are complex. It's not as simple as creating architectural drawings, securing all the building materials, and throwing together some bricks and mortars. The difficulties in building an internal HOME revolve around managing all the layers of biological, intellectual, psychological, and sociological rubbish that constitutes our daily "bread." It takes a great deal of effort. Each layer represents a higher degree of difficulty. It's like playing video games (artificial life)—moving to the next level requires mastering the level you are on. In real life, however, it's even more difficult: We have to confront multiple construction challenges in order to Be—it's a constant battle between the petty and the possible. Those construction challenges involved in building a HOME can be described as follows:

1. The DNA Challenge - confronting our genetic programming and biological make-up
2. The Instinct Challenge - confronting our base impulses of greed, lust, and envy.
3. The Thought Challenge - confronting old paradigms and beliefs
4. The Culture Challenge - confronting the norms of closed-mindedness and disingenuousness.
5. The Feeling Challenge - confronting our imagination, identification, and negative emotions.
6. The Spirit Challenge - confronting the distractions in our lives
7. The Purpose Challenge - confronting numbness and sleep

So, you might ask, who can be expected to confront challenges on seven fronts in order to build an internal HOME? The answer is a hard one:

- She who is committed to growth
- He who is willing to take on new challenges
- She who is ready for the effort
- He who believes it's the only thing that matters
- She who is able to live without recognition or reward
- He who is willing to see and to suffer
- She who can distinguish between form and force

This chapter explores the dynamics of each construction challenge and the strategies for dealing with all of them. The concluding section looks at the possibilities that life might present to us if we can optimize the events of daily life and connect with the intersection of our higher selves—our HOME. The ultimate challenge is to replace the petty with the possible.

A word of caution: Even if we were willing to make the necessary effort to confront the seven challenges, it will only prepare us for the possibility to be. Consciousness cannot be obtained by forcing the issues. We only invite the issue to be more of an intruder in our HOME. We may only get fleeting glimpses of its force by letting go of our egos and habits and by observing the desires of our three independently functioning centers: body, mind, and sensation.

One of my primary sources of wisdom, George I. Gurdjieff, suggests there are seven levels of development. Gurdjieff was an influential spiritual teacher of the early to mid-20th century who taught that most humans live their lives in a state of hypnotic "waking sleep", but that it is possible to transcend to a higher state of consciousness and achieve full human potential. Gurdjieff developed a method for doing so, calling his discipline "The Work."

At different times in his life, Gurdjieff formed and closed various schools around the world to teach the work. He claimed that the teachings he brought to the West from his own experiences and early travels expressed the truth found in ancient religions and wisdom teachings relating to self awareness in people's daily lives and humanity's place in the universe. Gurdjieff claimed that people cannot perceive reality in their current states because they do not possess consciousness but rather live in a state of a hypnotic "waking sleep." The seven levels of development are:

- Physical
- Intellectual
- Emotional
- Balanced
- Unified
- Conscious
- Perfected

The goal is to develop sufficient balance across the physical, intellectual, and emotional centers so that we can make possible moments of opportunity for unification and consciousness—soulful moments.

The DNA challenge and Instinct challenge constitute the battleground for the physical center. The Thought challenge and Culture challenge represent the battleground for the intellectual center. The Feeling challenge is directed toward the emotional center. The Spirit and Purpose challenges comprise the material to achieve some level of balance. All challenges are required to experience momentary sensations of being unified and conscious—to be at HOME. Perfection is not a possibility in our current state.

Hopefully, over time and with great effort, these soulful moments crystallize into a HOME. That process requires impartial objectivity, confronting these seven challenges simultaneously, letting go of our egos, and sensing our nothingness.

I resist willingness and readiness and I'm not able to do any of it in my current state. But I still find the challenges worth the effort. Do you? Then read on. Be here now, for a moment.

The DNA Challenge—
confronting our genetic programming

For better or for worse, we are stuck with our genetic constitution. Our biological make-up can make life easier for us or harder for us. We may have a strong skeletal and muscular structure that makes physical activity pleasurable, or one that makes it painful. We may have a brain that produces the right amount of dopamine, or not. It is what it is.

In the journal *Psychological Science*, neuroscientists report that extraverts tend to have a larger-than-average orbitofrontal cortex, a region that sits behind the eyes and is especially active when the brain registers rewards. Colin DeYoung, the study's lead author, says that extraverts have more machinery to keep track of winning. We either have the machinery for extraversion or we don't. Scientists have also found that very self-disciplined people tend to have a large lateral pre-fontal cortex, enabling them to plan ahead, parse through complex thoughts and make decisions. Similarly, people who often have negative, depressing thoughts tend to have a smaller medial prefrontal cortex, a part of the brain known to regulate emotion.

What this research suggests is that no matter how hard we may strive to develop our spiritual health, the simple fact is that we are stuck with the biological make-up with which we were born. If I want to be a brain surgeon, but have an IQ of 80, it is unlikely that I will be successful. These facts should not be used as an excuse to give up or to hide behind our limitations. We all have physical limitations. The important thing is to recognize and accept our DNA and observe how it plays out in our lives. There is no judgment or reason to feel sad, guilty, or vain. Our DNA is what it is.

Similarly, we are stuck with our size and, except for cosmetic machinations, our appearance. There is not much we can do to alter the fact that we are seven feet tall or five feet tall. And, unfortunately, people react differently to those of us who are exceptionally large or exceptionally small. If your goal is to be a professional basketball player and you are 5 feet 2 inches, it is unlikely that you are going to succeed.

The same is true for appearance. American media constantly glorifies tall, skinny, blonde woman and tall, muscular men. Indeed, our culture is more enamored by form than force, more by "false personality" than by essence. If your goal is to be a movie actress and your appearance doesn't happen to meet the artificially imposed standards of beauty in your culture, then it is unlikely you are going to be successful. It's just the way it is.

Given the facts about our biology and our body, it is a mistake to define ourselves by these variables. We need to understand them, accept them, and focus on who we can be independent of what we look like or what we are made of.

Possibilities for Being at HOME:

1. Know your own body
2. Accept your hard-wiring
3. Manage your biology

Know your own body. In my family, there is depression, schizophrenia, Tourette syndrome, diabetes, and Down syndrome. These physiological imbalances require attention and care. Not taking into account how physiology can affect outlook, performance, and energy would lead to an inaccurate explanation of how we think, feel, and act. Without an accurate diagnosis, it is folly to pursue our purpose and dreams. It is critically important to know our own biological barriers and assets. We need to know our physical limits and possibilities. We need to know how different foods affect our metabolism and well-being; for example, I have to avoid caffeine and sugar. If I consume too much, I feel jittery and tense. I know I feel more relaxed if I exercise regularly and get enough sleep. We need to know what our body needs in order to maximize energy as well as to be calm and still.

Accept your hard-wiring. Once I know my own body, I need to accept its strengths and limitations. For example, I have a high metabolism, which means that maintaining my weight is easier for me than it may be for others. I also have limitations: I have arthritis, which has caused me to have three hip replacements and has necessitated that I reduce my physical activities.

No matter what a person's physical make-up may be, the important challenge is to accept it for what it is. We can wish we had different bodies or biological constitutions as much as we want, but wishing our bodies were different won't change them. We have to play the hand we have been dealt and not let it play us.

<u>Manage your biology.</u> I am what I am. But while I can't change my biology, I can change my attitude toward my body and my biology, and I can change the way I manage my physiological givens. If I have diabetes, I have to be vigilant about what I eat, when I eat, and how much I exercise. I also need to keep track of my blood sugar to ensure that the steps I am taking are having the desired results. If I suffer from depression, I need to make sure I'm on the right medication and that I get the counseling I need. For me, Tourette syndrome is an irritating nuisance that I wish I didn't have. It's a literal pain in the neck for me, and a figurative pain in the neck for people close to me. I have to accept the fact that I have it, use my excess dopamine to my advantage, and do what I can through meditation and relaxation to reduce the tics. Everyone has physiological or biological issues they need to manage. We either choose to confront the challenge with ourselves or be defined by what we can't change.

The Instinct Challenge—confronting our base impulses of greed, lust, and envy

Gurdjieff concludes that human history can be summarized as "three-brained beings who reproduce on the planet earth and who engage in reciprocal destruction." This bleak view of the human condition suggests that humans have powerful instincts to engage in sexual relations and to kill people who threaten them in any of a number of ways—militarily, theologically, intellectually, etc. The instincts to exert power over others sexually, militarily, or intellectually have caused endless wars and suffering and continue to plague us today. Wilhelm Reich would say that our biggest plague is a lack of love for each other.

Apparently, humans also have instincts to form social communities. In *Guns, Germs, and Steel*, Jared Diamond describes the various levels of societal organization and how they affect our behavior:

The *Band*: Usually from 5 to 80 people blood-related and nomadic with one language and ethnicity, an egalitarian government, informal leadership, no bureaucracy, no formal structures for conflict resolution, and no economic specialization (e.g., Bushmen, pygmies).

The *Tribe:* Typically hundreds of people, often fixed settlements, consisting of kin-based clans with one ethnicity and language, egalitarian government, informal and often difficult conflict resolution problems (e.g., much of New Guinea, Amazonia).

Chiefdoms: Usually thousands of people in one or more villages with class and residence relationships, one ethnicity, centralized often hereditary rule, centralized conflict resolution, redistributive economy, intensive food production, early division of labor, and luxury goods (e.g., Polynesia, sub-Saharan Africa, etc.).

States: Typically 50,000 people with many villages and a capital, class-based relationships, one or more languages and ethnicities, centralized government, many levels of bureaucracy, monopolies of force and information, formalized laws and judges, intensive food production, division of labor, taxes, and public architecture.

States are especially good at developing weapons of war, providing troops, promoting religious fanaticism and patriotic fervor that makes troops willing to fight. States arise not just from the natural tendency of man (as Aristotle suggested), but by social contract, in response to needs for irrigation, and regional population size.

Government officials maintain power by disarming the populace and arming the elite, making the masses happy by redistributing some of the wealth, keeping order, curbing violence, promoting religion and ideology that justifies their power (and that promotes self-sacrifice on behalf of others), building public works, etc.

Within all of these groups, the instincts to reproduce, justify feeling superior, exert control over others, and destroy perceived enemies continually raise their ugly heads. This section is about how we confront those instincts and recognize the powerful social conditioning we have experienced over a very long period of time.

The instinct challenge is distinct from the DNA war. The DNA challenge has to do with how we deal intra-personally with our genes and biological make-up. The instinct war has to do with the relative importance of heredity and evolutionary forces in the nature of human interaction. Fields including evolutionary biology, psychology, and anthropology have expanded rapidly as researchers have come to show the importance of inborn characteristics on behavior.

Here are some useful facts about how we have evolved:

- The Universe was formed about 14 billion years ago with the Big Bang.
- Our solar system and earth were formed about 5 billion years ago through planetary collisions.
- Microscopic life appeared about 4 billion years ago in the sea.
- Multi-cellular organisms appeared about 1 billion years ago.
- Animals emerged onto land about 400 million years ago.
- Apes descended from trees about 7 million years ago.
- Pre-historic humans evolved about 2.5 million years ago.
- Modern humans evolved in Africa about 130,000 years ago.
- Final fact: Only 14% of Americans believe the facts above and this percentage has not changed significantly over the last 30 years even though science has made incredible leaps.

We are the products of evolution and natural selection. In order to survive, we acquired instincts, as members of different sized groups, that still affect our behavior today even though the instincts no longer serve any useful purpose.

Our instincts for greed, lust, envy, and swagger have been conditioned over a very long period of time. What's important is to recognize how these instincts are present in our lives and to observe how behaviors associated with them play out in our lives. On a hopeful note, it appears that psychological evolution may also be occurring particularly in regard to our empathic capabilities. If true, this is a very hopeful trend because learning to relate constructively with each other may be the most important factor in our survival as a planet.

Possibilities for being at HOME:

1. Investigate the power of evolution
2. Identify your primal instincts
3. Manage your instincts

<u>Investigate the power of evolution</u>. Instincts have played a major role in how humans evolved over the past 130,000 years. And our primal past perseveres in the present. Let's start, however, with acknowledging the impossible improbability of being here in the first place. When I stop to think how many random iterations it took over 4 billion years for me to be here now, I'm struck with a deep gratitude for my existence and my possibilities.

Instincts that may have been useful and necessary to survive our tribal history are no longer helping us preserve our planet. We needed clubs to defend ourselves from violent intrusions by neighboring tribes and/or predatory animals. We needed strong sex drives to produce enough children to sustain population growth during periods of plague and pestilence. Unfortunately, our clubs have evolved to nuclear weapons and our sex drives have created a lucrative reward system for modern day slavery. Paradoxically, the instincts that may have accounted for our survival may now lead to our extinction. We need to understand the power of these instincts, how they evolved, and whether or not they are still functional.

Identify your primal instincts. Take an inventory of your primal instincts. Which ones play a dominant role in your behavior? Do you have strong physical instincts such as lust; strong emotional instincts such as envy, vanity, or greed; or strong intellectual instincts such as thinking you are superior or finding what's wrong with everyone else but you? Which of your instincts or impulses emanate from your lower centers and which ones from your higher centers?

Manage your instincts. Observing our instincts can be an opportunity to identify what drives our behavior. The idea is to see and to suffer—to see how our instincts rule our lives without being conscious of them, and to suffer from the shame of being less than we could be and doing less than we are able for the good of others. Being able to observe our vanity, superiority, pride, negativity, lust, greed, and envy gives us a chance to make choices—to manage how we are going to act and who we are going to be.

The Thought Challenge—
confronting old paradigms and beliefs

Our thoughts and beliefs are so conditioned by our needs for security and certainty that we have a very difficult time opening up to new possibilities for our lives and to the unknown. Our behaviors and our conclusions are based on our beliefs. Our beliefs are typically not based on solid evidence that is established through rigorous inquiry into the highest quality and enormous quantity of research, science, and history available to us. We cling to our beliefs with ferocious intensity and react violently when they are questioned or come under attack.

Many psychologists have built their therapeutic models on a rational approach to confronting beliefs that result in self-defeating or destructive behaviors. One model, developed by Albert Ellis, takes an ABCDE path to therapy:

Antecedent
Belief
Consequence
Dispute
Effect

The **antecedent** is a triggering event that we think is responsible for a particular **consequence.** For example, a car pulls out in front of us (**antecedent)** and we have to slam on the brakes causing us to feel angry and yell obscenities (**consequence).** Ellis argues that it is not the fact of the car pulling out that causes our reaction, but our **beliefs** about that event that cause us to react as we do. Those beliefs might include:

"That person is an ignorant jerk whose intention was to get ahead of me and make me mad."
"I shouldn't have to put up with rude behavior."
"It's not fair that I have to slow down just because that person was in a rush."
"If only I had the road to myself."

These beliefs, not the event, are what caused the reaction. The path forward, according to Ellis, would be to **dispute** those beliefs and substitute them with a healthier set of beliefs. For example, the person who reacted may have made an assumption that wasn't true. While the other driver's behavior was not acceptable, the intention was probably not to make the other driver mad. The reality of life is that some people can be rude and that life is not fair. And, clearly, it is wishful thinking to believe that we should have the road to ourselves. Theoretically, accepting the realities of the world in which we live and confronting our own irrational beliefs has the **effect** of living a less stressful and more rational life, hence—Rational Emotive Therapy, an essential construct for dealing with the thought challenge.

The thought challenge, therefore, is to confront our own conditioning and irrational beliefs and to inquire deeply into the underlying foundation of our belief systems. We don't like to do that.

The challenge involves putting to bed our ordinary intelligence in order to awaken a new intelligence.

Possibilities for Being at HOME:

1. Observe your thoughts and beliefs
2. Challenge those thoughts and beliefs with active inquiry and scholarly sources
3. Open yourself to thinking differently

Observe your thoughts and beliefs. Thoughts happen. The only question is whether or not we observe them as they occur. There is no need for guilt or anxiety about any thought you may have. You just need to observe the thought and ask, "Where did that come from, why am I thinking this way, and is there another way to think about this that may be more useful?" We develop our thoughts and beliefs based on our experiences growing up in whatever social, political, or religious environment we happen to land—either by choice or by accident. If I were born into a Muslim family in Saudi Arabia, it's pretty likely that I would espouse Islamic teaching of one sort or another. If I were born into a hippy family in the '60s, it's likely that I would have a liberal perspective on the world. Independent of our social, political, or religious histories, however, we need to observe and articulate the thoughts and beliefs we hold dear, ask where they came from, and consider constructive alternatives.

<u>Challenge your thoughts and beliefs with active inquiry and scholarly sources.</u> Everyone has the right to believe what they want to believe, but I believe everyone has the responsibility to examine the sources of those beliefs with diligence, rigor, and an open mind. If I believe that Joseph Smith received the latest revelations in tablets from an angel and then the angel returned to heaven with the tablets, then I have responsibility to inquire deeply about the validity of those claims and I need to examine closely the lifestyle this Joseph Smith promoted. That same level of inquiry is required for whatever religious or political belief I may have. We are all believers; we just believe different things. What's important is to actively expand the quantity of references and rigorously analyze the quality of our sources.

<u>Open yourself to thinking differently.</u> One of the biggest blinders to an open mind is the extent to which we identify with a particular ethnic group, nationality, religion, or political party. We need to shed ourselves of any labels that limit our thinking. And we need to open ourselves to exploring issues with multi-dimensional thinking. Any event or situation can be viewed from multiple angles with shades of nuance. We need to free ourselves from limiting labels and empower ourselves with tools and constructs for processing information in meaningful ways. Only then can we cut through all the external influences

and connect with who we are at our core. Thinking frees us to be who we are.

The Culture Challenge—confronting the norms of closed-mindedness and disingenuousness

There are 3 things to know about culture:

1. Culture has a profound effect on our behavior.
2. We are largely unaware of how we are conditioned by culture.
3. We can create norms of our own choosing.

If you don't think culture has a huge impact on behavior, then recall the prevalence of past practices that were considered normal. For example, Chinese families used to bind their daughters' feet, often resulting in lifelong physical disability. Or consider that genital cutting still occurs in several cultures to reduce the probability that young women will engage in pre-marital sex. Imagine growing up in Pakistan where, in 2010, only 1% of the children ended up going to college. Wouldn't this lack of education limit the possibilities you might consider? Or think about what it might be like to grow up in a remote African village in which the average income is $1 per day. Wouldn't that level of poverty make survival your only focus? Consider how growing up in an American Southern Baptist family might influence the way you view spirituality. Wouldn't the literal and fundamental beliefs make it difficult for you to seek God within, to see women as central, and to see Jesus as a human parable who modeled what was possible for all of us?

Kids who grow up in Muslim societies and are educated in a Madrassa are unlikely to be encouraged to engage in inquiry or to be open to new possibilities. Most kids who grow up in America are preoccupied with money, materialism, and militarism because that's what they hear in their homes, what they see in the media, and what they can't avoid in their schools. American kids are inundated with the petty points of life: celebrity, fame, and fashion. These cultural influences impact how they see themselves and how they view the world.

We are bombarded with messages from the cultures in which we live. These messages exert an enormous influence on our thoughts, feelings, and sensations. Recognizing the effects of cultural norms on our beliefs and behaviors is very difficult to do on our own. This is one reason why Gurdjieff suggests that finding new possibilities in our lives requires special schools that facilitate self awareness and encourage efforts to grow.

What is important here is to identify the norms that influence our behavior and to ask ourselves if those are the norms we would choose for ourselves given who we are. If they aren't, we can either try to change the norms or find a community that has a different set of norms, values, beliefs, expectations, and rewards.

Possibilities for Being at HOME:

1. Engage in respectful dialogue
2. Create norms of your own choosing
3. Enable community ownership.

<u>Engage in respectful dialogue.</u> If you decide you want to change the norms in your environment, it is critical to engage in respectful dialogue with the people who make up that environment. The environment consists of people with different DNA, different instincts, and different thoughts and

beliefs ingrained over a long period of time. People do not particularly embrace change, and they don't welcome anyone who tries to impose changes on them. I know I don't. Therefore, as a starting point, there has to be a willingness to engage in respectful dialogue—which means paying attention to what's important, listening carefully, demonstrating understanding to what people are saying, and finding a reason why other people might want to listen to your point of view. It may require collaboration, compromise, and concession on some points. It starts with greeting people of difference with a welcoming tone, posture, and attitude. Then, it's simply a matter of demonstrating genuine interest in the other person's point of view, and trying to summarize your understanding of what that person is saying or feeling. Finally, it's perfectly acceptable to provide your point of view in a rational and non-inflammatory way being sensitive to words or behaviors that might offend the other person.

<u>Create norms of your own choosing.</u> We are a product of history and habits. Our customary responses to the world are conditioned reactions to a given stimulus. We have a choice to make. According to Robert Carkhuff, one of the most cited social scientists of the last century, there are five levels of responses (R) to the stimuli (S) we encounter in our respective cultures:

Reactions/ Responses	Processing Orientation	Implication
S-R	None	We simply react habitually to any stimulus that occurs—there is no real thinking, only culturally conditioned responses acquired during our history on this planet.

S-O-R	Discriminating Organism	We (Organism) make discriminations about the right response from our repertoire of responses in our given culture.
S-P-R	Thinking Person	We process information (P) and generate new individual responses to changing cultural conditions.
S-OP-R	Organizational Context	We process organizational information (OP) and generate new organizational responses to changing cultural conditions and standards.
S-CP-R	Cultural Context	We process cultural information (CP) and create new cultural conditions and standards.

If we want to create norms of our own choosing, we have to think differently by processing cultural information and creating new cultural conditions, standards, and traditions. We have to engage with others to decide on the kind of cultural environment we want to create. That means defining the values, norms, expectations, behaviors, and rewards that distinguish one culture from another.

Enable community ownership. To reform cultures and traditions, we have to change the shared commitments of a community. If we respectfully engage and provide meaningful processing constructs to the people in our communities, we may make a temporary impact. For sustained change, however, the people in the community need to take ownership of the changes and make a commitment to the desired norms and values.

The Feeling Challenge—
confronting our imagination, identification, and negative emotions

We experience a vast range of emotions in highly differentiated levels of intensity as part of our daily lives. Most of them go unnoticed by ourselves and others. The following chart illustrates the range and intensity of feelings we may experience in a given day:

	Up	Down	Anger	Fear	Confusion
High Intensity					
Medium Intensity					
Low Intensity					

A high intensity "up" word might be ecstatic or thrilled. A medium intensity "confusion" word might be torn or conflicted. These feelings occur in response to changing conditions in our lives. We may start out the day feeling happy because we got a good night's sleep and the sun is shining. When we get in our car and discover the battery is dead, our light-hearted mood may suddenly turn dark. We might feel angry and exasperated because the last person who drove the car left the light on and now we are going to be late for an important meeting. Most of the feelings we experience on a daily basis are a reaction to petty events that happen randomly in our lives.

What we want to feel is compassion, calmness, love, peace, and passion to be. Instead, we react negatively to anything that threatens our sense of identity. As a result, we spend too much of our lives in the down, anger, fear, and confusion categories.

Most of our lives are dominated by our DNA, our instincts, our thoughts, and cultural norms. These constitute the physical and intellectual aspects of our lives. In order to have any chance of being whole and balanced, we need to be awake to our sensations, feelings, and emotions. We can't be present or feel unified without full consciousness of our feelings, but our physical centers and intellectual centers command most of our attention. Our physical center drags us one way, our intellectual center insists on another way, and meanwhile our emotional center scrambles to get in the game. And these centers are all constantly reacting to ordinary events in our ordinary lives. The higher centers, to whatever extent they may exist, are asleep, unconscious, and out of play. We can't hope to gain any access to these higher centers if our feelings are not in the game—not a full part of our daily lives. Our feelings and sensations are essential prerequisites for bringing our physical and intellectual centers into balance and for giving ourselves any chance of relating to our higher selves.

Possibilities for Being at HOME:

1. Observe your feelings
2. Choose your actions
3. Understand the consequences of your choices

Observe your feelings. Just like thoughts, feelings happen. The only question is: Do we observe them as they occur? There is no need for guilt or anxiety about any feeling you may have. You just need to observe the feeling and ask, "Where did that come from, and why am I feeling this way?" It does take effort to stay awake to our feelings because our physical and intellectual centers are demanding attention as they react to ordinary events. We may feel a sexual urge and urgently look for ways to satisfy it. We may have a big presentation at work that demands all our attention and energy. Ordinary life keeps calling. Feelings get lost in the noise. Our first step is to fight to stay awake to the feelings and sensations we are having as we navigate our lives; and remember, we are not our body, mind, or feelings—we are spiritual beings with physical, emotional, and intellectual centers.

Choose your actions. Feelings do not give us permission to act any way we want. Feeling murderous does not mean we are free to kill someone. Feeling sexually attracted to someone doesn't give us the right to force ourselves on a man or woman who captures our fancy. We can choose how we act on our feelings, but having a choice presupposes that we are aware of the feelings we are having. When our physical, emotional, and intellectual centers are in balance, it is much easier to make healthy choices. When we are in touch at any level with our centers, we are far more likely to make constructive, soul enhancing choices. We can choose.

Understand the consequences of your choices. Our choices have consequences. If we decide to avoid old friends because we are envious of their lives, then we may destroy a bridge to a meaningful relationship. If we hurt someone because we are angry with them, we may end up in jail. On the other hand, if we are able to be conscious, calm, and compassionate in whatever situation we find ourselves, we are more likely to feel at peace with ourselves and create a more potent inner force. Feelings are the pathways to our higher selves. If we listen with our heart instead of our head, we hear messages at a deeper level. We form more soulful connections with ourselves and others. We are more present. If we simply attend physically and listen intellectually, we miss the nuances and richness of what we are hearing from others and what we are observing in our inner dialogue. When we don't observe our feelings and sense our emotions, we remain asleep and fragmented.

The Spirit Challenge— confronting the distractions in our lives

The world in which we live constantly calls for our attention. We need to make money, make friends, make decisions. We must react to events that demand a response. The boss calls and asks why your project is late. The spouse calls and asks you to pick up the kids. The car stalls and needs repair. The bill collector sends you a letter saying your payment is past due.

We want to be centered. We want to be unified. We want to awake. We want to be balanced. We want to be present—physically, emotionally, and intellectually. But we are not. We are so caught up in the trappings, illusions, and demands of our ordinary lives, that we lose track of who we are. We have so much to do there is no time to be. We are so attached to the forms of life that we lose track of the force of life.

These distractions are real and constant. We are constantly bombarded by the media. One purpose of the media is to make money. They make money and get ratings by entertaining us and sensationalizing the latest "breaking news." And they are successful. We spend more time observing and listening to news events, sports events, and entertainment sources than we spend observing and listening to ourselves. The sad fact is that most American kids spend more time watching TV in the first 18 years of their lives than they spend in the classroom. Screen time on other electronic devices has compounded the problem. This has not only resulted in a decline in educational achievement, but also in a decline of spiritual fulfillment.

And, as in a progressive video game, the challenges are getting harder. Confronting the physical challenges by managing our DNA and instincts can be fairly easy—it is simply the price of entry. Confronting the intellectual challenges by disputing our beliefs and creating healthy environments ups the ante. Confronting the emotional challenges by being conscious of feelings and making better choices raises the stakes further. To confront the spiritual challenge means achieving a balance among our physical, intellectual, emotional, and spiritual centers and making the effort to unify and be conscious—even for a moment. This challenge is not about proving others' ideological beliefs are wrong; it is not about convincing ourselves that our beliefs are superior; it is about finding opportunities to spark our consciousness and connect to the God within and the divine spark above.

Possibilities for Being at HOME:

1. Recognize your identification, imagination, and negative emotions
2. Resist the temptation to give in
3. Relate your lower centers to your higher centers

Recognize your identification, imagination, and negative emotions. The spirit challenge starts by recognizing what gets in the way of our path to growth, development, and increased Presence. Identification is one major hurdle on the path to

Presence. Identification means that we define ourselves by our ethnicity, nationality, religion, political affiliation, or role (e.g. parent, psychologist, teacher, doctor, lawyer, executive, etc.). By defining ourselves through external labels, we limit our ability to expand ourselves through internal consciousness.

Imagination is the second hurdle on the path to Presence. Imagination means that we delude ourselves into thinking we are more than we are. The most egregious examples are movie stars, deceptive politicians, and corrupt business tycoons who think their celebrity status gives their opinions weight and substance. Because they are so addicted to adulation and so convinced of their importance, they have a difficult time connecting with their nothingness. Knowing we are nothing on this random rock in the universe with over 7 billion human inhabitants is the essential starting point for spiritual growth.

Negative emotion is the third hurdle on the path to Presence. Negative emotion means that we feel cheated, bitter, depressed, or angry (or any number of useless, soul sucking emotions) because the world has not given us what we think we deserve. Letting go of negative emotions means we give up our "what ifs," "if onlys," and "woulda-shoulda-couldas" and realize that life is not fair and that our only real choice is to see everything that happens as spiritual bread. The ugly truth is that random events happen with no particular reason. We simply need to view whatever happens as an opportunity to dig deeper and observe more closely how we respond to any twist or turn in life's journey. And to find meaning in whatever happens to us—positive or negative.

<u>Resist the temptation to give in</u>. It is so easy to get caught in the flow of life and not make the effort to lift our heads out of the

water to look around for the possibilities that are continually unfolding in front of us. There are boundless opportunities to jump into the stream and get carried swiftly through life until, all too suddenly, we get dumped into the ocean of death with very few moments of consciousness along the way. We need to resist identification, imagination, and negative emotions—not by judging ourselves, but by observing how often we are in these states and accepting the fact that while these temptations may define our human condition they do not need to define our spiritual possibilities.

<u>Relate your lower centers to your higher centers</u>. Finally we come to the ultimate challenge—connecting our lower centers to our higher centers. Unfortunately, I don't have a clue how to do this. Theoretically, I know the first step is to achieve some level of unification of the physical, emotional and intellectual centers. The second step is to develop moments of consciousness in which there is some connection with our higher centers. The third step is to somehow relate the lower to the higher making the higher centers active and the lower centers passive. And the last step is to establish a crystallized essence or Presence that sits beside the higher and lower centers—our inner God. My feeble attempts to connect to the higher centers and to relate to lower centers come through meditation during which I receive fleeting glimpses of what may be possible. Since my lower centers are way too active, I am not unified, and I am rarely awake or conscious at any level, I am totally unqualified to provide any substantive or experiential guidance for this challenge. I can only share what I have gleaned through my reading and the conclusions I have reached through my lower intellectual. To complicate matters further, I know that trying to relate lower centers to higher centers and establish a Presence beside them through my

intellectual center can be a barrier and will not achieve my goal. I believe that meditation and qigong are the best strategies, but I don't know how to make them real. I can only continue to practice both and make efforts to be at HOME.

The Purpose Challenge— confronting numbness and sleep

My purposes are to awake, to unify, to be present, and to heal. Unfortunately, I am asleep most of the time, fragmented all the time, rarely present, and I have no capability to heal. I am nothing. I am where I am and I am exactly where I need to be to confront my challenges and pursue my purpose.

The purpose challenge is all about observing numbness and sleep—being numb to all the impressions around us and being asleep most of our lives. Being asleep simply means not being fully awake, not being conscious, and not being present for ourself or others. As we have seen in all the previous chapters, this is no simple matter because we are confronting challenges on six other fronts while we are trying to fight this one.

In her amazing book, *The Reality of Being*, Jeanne de Salzmann, a student of Gurdjieff for over 40 years, distills the real meaning of purpose in these powerful words:

> In order for me to pass beyond fragmentation, this separation from my essential being, all the energy in me needs to blend. It needs to be entirely liberated. For this, an absolute tranquility needs to appear in all the parts of myself. This is not in order to succeed, or to receive and appropriate to myself something marvelous. Rather, it is to see my nothingness,

my attachment, my fear of losing the meaning I attribute to myself. Instead of always wanting to be right, I see my contradictions. I see myself hypnotized by my imagination. I see everything together, both my ego and the real "I." In so seeing, I liberate myself. For a moment I am no longer the same. My freed attention, my consciousness, then knows what I am essentially. This is the death of my ordinary "I." To remember oneself means to die to oneself, to the lie of one's imagination. In remembering oneself, it is the letting go of the ego that allows a new consciousness to penetrate. Then I see that the ordinary "I" is a phantom, a projection of myself. In fact, everything I take as manifestation is not something separate, but a projection of the essential. Returning to the source, I become conscious of that which arises not to fall back, that which is not born and does not die—the eternal self."

To me, those words describe purpose far better than what I could even begin to express. Our purpose is to let our ordinary "I" die in order to let our eternal, essential self emerge.

Possibilities for Being at HOME:

1. Identify your values and what gives you meaning
2. Dedicate yourself to living those values
3. Observe desires that are incompatible with your purpose

<u>Identify your values and what gives you meaning</u>. Just as there are physical, intellectual, emotional, and spiritual wars there are also values for each. We all have different values and

weight those values differently. Here are some values that are important to me in each of those four areas:

Physical Values: Health, energy, strength, endurance, financial security, beautiful living environment, private working environment, access to cultural events

Emotional Values: Relationship with wife and children, respect, friends, honesty, integrity, fairness, compassion, being positive

Intellectual Values: Challenge, variety, multi-dimensional thinking, elegance, simplicity, rigor, substance, scholarship, congruence

Spiritual Values: Connectedness, community, calmness, consciousness, unity

You probably have different values or put more importance on some values than others. What's important is to identify what they are and their level of importance, because they become your individual objectives and, in totality, your purpose.

Dedicate yourself to living those values. Once we have defined and weighted our values, we can assess how well we are doing with each one. We can determine the degree of congruence between what we say is important and how we act on a day-to-day basis. We can ask ourselves how much effort we make in satisfying each of the values and what degree of urgency we assign to each value. For me, asking those questions gives me a temporary shock that helps me wake up . . . . for a moment. Based on a brutally honest assessment, we can re-dedicate ourselves to what we say is important—to our defined purpose.

<u>Observe desires that are incompatible with your purpose</u>. What is true in confronting all the previous challenges is true in confronting this one: the most valuable commitment we can make is to observe ourselves in the moment. In this case, we observe the congruence, or lack thereof, of our values and actions. By making this observation, and not going into a judgmental hole that only creates negative energy, we put ourselves in position to accept our human frailties and to make effort toward our spiritual possibilities.

THE PROCESS

In my search of the literature and my experience practicing qigong, I keep finding four key behaviors of people who are spiritually evolved. It seems to me that we will know we have arrived at HOME when we comfortably and consistently practice these behaviors:

- Love All
- Let Go
- Open Up
- Let In

<u>Love All</u>

Loving all means inviting everyone into our HOME regardless of differences. It means creating space for others and welcoming them into the world. Loving all is more than tolerance, it is full acceptance and inclusion. Loving all requires us to forgive whatever happened in the past and to reach out to people outside our regular boundaries.

The key is to be able to imagine the Ideal End State and then assume that we are already there. We simply need to pay conscious attention to where we are in the moment. Instead of trying to become more open, forgiving, accepting, and loving, we assume that those attributes describe the essence of who we are. We assume that we live in that HOME instead of travelling toward it.

Let Go

Letting go means freeing ourselves from ego and desire. Buddhists would describe this as non-attachment. We can let go of our need for fame, fortune, and recognition—our need to be the center of attention. We can let go of our envy, greed, and lust—our need to be the best, get the most, and satisfy every whim.

Letting go also entails an acceptance that some of our long held beliefs and positions of certainty might not necessarily be true. People who are particularly self righteous have a difficult time admitting they are wrong or letting go of their superior attitude. Letting go of bitterness and hate from one form of mistreatment or another is another healing act. Forgiveness can help us let go of past grudges or resentments.

Open Up:

Opening Up means to actively explore physical, emotional, intellectual, and spiritual possibilities. It is the opposite of willful ignorance in which people refuse to consider any facts or experiences that run counter to their established beliefs. In *Thinking Fast and Slow*, Daniel Kahneman, a Nobel Prize-winning professor, discusses the results of 40 years of research in the way we think. In short, System 1 thinkers look for stories to support their beliefs, and System 2 thinkers rigorously analyze evidence in search of the truth. All of us have some combination of System 1 and System 2 tendencies. The problem is that we are less likely to engage our System 2 thinking methods because it takes too much work and we are essentially lazy. Plus, we are all believers and we all look for stories to support our beliefs. We just believe different things and look for different stories to support those beliefs.

Kahneman's research sheds new perspective on the problems we are facing in the world today. If everyone continues to adhere rigidly to their particular set of beliefs and remain closed to any ideas or information that do not support those beliefs, we are in deep trouble. Just take into account this approximate distribution of people in the world who subscribe to the various religions:

Christians:	2.1 billion
Muslims:	1.8 billion
Hindus:	1 billion
Buddhists:	500 million
Other religions:	500 million
Jews:	14 million

Add up the numbers and you will find that about 6 billion of the 7 billion people on earth subscribe to some kind of religious belief. Many of these religious beliefs provide profound insight and helpful guidance for navigating our individual journeys. The problem is that a large share of religious people are fairly certain they are right and that all the others are wrong. The same, of course, is true of the 1 billion secularists who are equally convinced about the certainty of their beliefs. My point is that as long as we remain closed and insular, we are unlikely to see any breakthroughs either as a civil society or as enlightened individuals. Opening up means breaking through the closed conditioning of our pasts. It means looking for possibilities and wonder in every moment. But that's just the first step.

On a physical level, we can open our meridians to improve energy flow. On an emotional level, we can open our hearts to embrace more people. On an intellectual level, we can open our minds to explore new ideas. On a spiritual level, we can open our souls to universal energy, cosmic connection, ultimate mystery, and profound possibility.

<u>Let In</u>

Letting in means being willing to accept unconditional love. In the film, *The Perks of Being a Wallflower*, the teacher says to one of his students: "You attract the love you think you deserve." If we don't love ourselves, we are unlikely to believe that others could love us. Sometimes, overcoming abusive childhood experiences makes it difficult to let love in. Letting love in when you believe you don't deserve it presents major challenges to people on their path.

Letting in even minimal amounts of love from the sentient beings on earth is difficult enough. Letting in the light, warmth, and love of the Universe requires a whole new level of acceptance. It requires acceptance of ourselves, acceptance of a nameless force and source operating in the world, and acceptance of the possibility of fulfillment beyond our imaginations.

For me, loving all is the most difficult. I do a fairly good job of opening up and letting in, but I struggle with letting go and I suck at loving all. Anger and impatience are still frequent intruders in my HOME.

ONE PATH TO BEING

In 1968. Apollo 11 landed the first humans on the moon. Neil Armstrong stepped onto the lunar surface and described the event as "one small step for a man, one giant leap for mankind." While Apollo 11 advanced our understanding of outer space, this book is intended to encourage readers to advance their understanding of inner space. Each person takes a different path to discover his or her individual HOME. Hopefully, some of the ideas in this book will help to pave the way to Being for you.

After 40 years of studying these ideas and living in the gap between what I know and who I am, I decided to take a small step in preparation for a giant leap into the great unknown. I thought about an ashram in India. I thought about a long trek in Tibet. I explored all kinds of options for finding my internal HOME.

Finally, I realized that my best course was to build on what I had already learned. Since I had been practicing qigong for 15 years and knew a master in China, I decided to find out what he was doing. As it turned out, he was offering month long retreats in

China. My decision was made. The following pages contain a brief overview of my learning from the experience.

I understand that a three-week retreat hardly compares to a two-year walk in the dessert or a five-year intensive internship with a spiritual guru. I am only sharing a peek into this experience, because I found it extremely useful and enlightening, and because it reveals some road markers on one path to Being. I am not claiming that this one experience qualifies me to be anything more than a happy participant in an enriching program. The highlights, however, should yield insights about what can happen even over a short period of time.

So bear with me as I bare my soul. At a minimum it should be worth a few laughs.

After a 15 hour flight to Hong Kong and one night in a hotel to recover before taking a ferry to China, I decided to start my day with mediation and QiGong. Figured I might as well get into the swing of things. I have tried to start each day with meditation and QiGong for the past 15 years or so, but I only manage to do it about 3-4 days per week. There were many years when I would go a week or two without either, so the practice is not exactly sacred or habitual. Habitual probably describes the practice all too well. I tended to go through the motions without a high level of consciousness. It was more words than sensations. Here are the words and their corresponding intention.

I am at One (We are all connected in the universe)
I am at peace (No matter what happens to me or around me, I
    accept it)

I am calm and still (I always maintain my equanimity)
I am here now (This is the eternal moment)

I can lighten my being (It's silly to take myself too seriously)
I can be kind (Everyone has their own pain—I need to be
   understanding and supportive)
I can extend love (As Reich would say, we suffer from an
   emotional plague. "All we need is love")
I can smile on the universe (No matter what happens to me or
   around me, I can use it as daily bread)

I wish to awake (I need to be more conscious of each moment)
I wish to unify (I need to find harmony among my PEIS centers)
I wish to heal (I want to have some impact on the violence and
   hate in the world)

I am a solid mountain (Nothing can shake me or rattle me—life
   events roll off me)
I am a warm sea (I am supportive and buoyant)
I am a free flower (I am creative and innovative)

Thank God for the earth (Thanks to universal energy, cosmic
   connection, ultimate mystery, and possibility love, I have a
   life on this random rock in the universe—it's an impossible
   improbability that I'm here)
Thank God for water (Without water nothing grows. With
   water, amazing possibilities are constantly unfolding in
   front of me)
Thank God for the sun. (It's miraculous that the earth is
   positioned at exactly the right distance from the sun to
   create a tolerable range of cold and heat)
Thank God for air (It's amazing that the air we breathe is able to
   sustain us)

Thank God for time (I am grateful for the opportunity to have lived for 68 years and counting)

Thank God for knowledge (I am grateful for the books and authors that have informed my thinking—Gurdjieff, Reich, Nietzsche, Carkhuff and all their associates)

Thank God for space (I am grateful for the universe and the galaxies that somehow got created and are mysterious sources of higher energy)

Thank God for light (I am grateful that when we die people experience a Light that warms that path—however it is created and to wherever it leads)

Thank God for thought (I am grateful that I am able to think, process, communicate, and innovate)

Thank God for sound (I am grateful for music and the sounds of nature)

Thank God for love (I'm grateful for my family and friends)

Thank God for hope (I'm grateful for the opportunity to grow and develop—to be different)

Thank God for senses (I'm grateful for my ability to see, hear, smell, taste, touch)

Thank God for roots (I'm grateful to have the loving, accepting, honest parents that I had)

Note: This is the mid-point of the meditation. A couple of things strike me. One, these words have very little congruence with my actual experience; and two, it only takes me about 15 minutes to go through this whole meditation (again, I'm only half way through). Gurus would probably suggest that each line requires 15 days of reflection, but I rush through the whole meditation in 15 minutes. This is totally an aspirational meditation. If only it actually conformed with who I am. What this meditation clearly illustrates is there is a huge gap between my knowledge and my being. I feel good and proud to be able to translate all the books I have read into a 15 minute summary. I feel exposed because it's just another example of being entirely in my head. I need to get these words to my heart. I need a stronger mind-body connection as well as a stronger connection to the real Source of transformation. Gurdjieff wrote a book, Life is Real Only Then, When "I Am"; Jeanne deSalzmann, one of Gurdjieff's students, wrote another related book, *The Reality of Being*. They did not mean, "I am real when I have words to express esoteric thoughts." I think they meant, "I am only real when I directly perceive and experience these sensations." For me, they are mostly words. My hope is that the retreat will help me experience them as real: direct perceptions, actual sensations.

Back to my meditation. After all, I have another 7.5 minutes to go.

At this point in my meditation, since I've been up and down my chakras twice, I introduce Kundalini Yoga into my meditation to enable me to go one more time up my Chakras in order to achieve the law of three and cram everything I know into one meditation. So here we go up the Chakras from the base of the spine to the top of the head—where I'm supposed to connect to higher energy. I actually use a chant indicated below, but I am still unable to connect.

Llllll aaaaaaaaa mmmmmm: Stay grounded in who I am
Vvvvvv aaaaaaaa mmmmmm: Observe envy, lust, and greed
Rrrrrr aaaaaaaa mmmmmm: Observe imagination, identification, and negative emotion.

Eeeeee aaaaaa mmmmmm: (Be open, honest, and direct)
Mmmmmmmmmmmmmm: (Listen to the voice of God—higher energy/higher self)

Oooohhhhhhhmmmmmmmm: (Think!)
No chant (Connect to a higher purpose, energy, source or force)

You will notice that each of the 3 times up and down the Chakras required 7 steps—the law of 7 and law of 3.

The problem is that I take this whole meditation very seriously, but I feel foolish because it doesn't seem to translate. It's not real because I don't have any clear sense of what "I Am" means.

Now I incorporate some Aikido principles of centering, weighting, and extending, which I learned from another friend. Long story.

Center (Put all my energy two inches below my navel)
Weight (Feel my eye lids getting heavy and I can't lift up my hands)
Extend (Send out positive energy to the universe)

Wheww!!! I'm almost done. Now, I simply try to relax and say 3 times each:

Just breathe (inhale on just, exhale on breathe)
Higher active, lower passive (try to connect with my higher self, e.g. compassion, love, forgiveness; and observe my lower self, e.g. impatience, intolerance, self-justification, self-deception etc.)

Finally, I do an exercise of putting conscious awareness on my right arm as I say, "I am," my right leg as I say "I am," my left leg as I say "I am," and my left arm as I say "I am." Of course, I do that 3 times and then focus on the base of my spine as I say, "I am," my solar plexus as I say, "I am," my chest as I say, "I am," and my head as I say, "I am." When I focus on my head I try to empty and quiet all of these racing thoughts just described and move the energy to my solar plexus where I say "I am." This is where I stay (for all of 30 seconds) in an attempt to 1) deepen my presence and 2) find a spot I can return to when someone needs me to be present.

I almost never remember to do that.

And this, in 15 minutes mind you, concludes my meditation. Now, in an attempt to make all those words "Real" and to translate them into "Sensation," I do my 15 minutes of Qi Gong. As I go through the form, here are the words I repeat throughout the process:

Lift Chi up, pull Chi down
Stillness in movement, movement in stillness
Open up the Possible, close down the petty
I am in the universe, the Universe is in me (energy exchange)

Sharing all of this makes me realize I should have titled this book, "An ADHD person's guide to spiritual transformation."

After arriving at the retreat center and completing the first day of training, I realized that the key concept on which to focus is the where, what, and how of our internal chi. The where is the lower abdomen. The what is release and absorb. The how is a constant turning. The turning is the critical piece and it's very difficult to do. Staying centered in the abdomen, consciously releasing and absorbing, and imagining the turning of the ball will take a lifetime to make less clumsy and conscious.

Thankfully, it turned out that Luke is the real thing. He is totally humble, gracious, generous, loving, patient, and compassionate. I couldn't have asked for a better, kinder teacher. He has made a real science of chi and is totally authentic—no ego, no airs, no pretending.

Each day consisted of several intense sessions culminating with a full one-hour exercise. The teaching focused on intention, conduction, and sensation. Luke explained how our bodies are like pulleys and how we need to use mind over muscle. The exercises definitely got me out of my head but it was far from a natural act.

This form of QiGong (ChiLel Qi Gong) is all about the ball in the abdomen. The ball orchestrates our energies and keeps us in rhythm with the universe. The experience forced me to focus all my energy on the abdomen instead of my head. I don't know how it compares with Gurdjieff's movements, but it feels like it's for the same intention. There is an emphasis on sensation so that when I release chi, I can feel it at my shoulder, my elbow and my wrist.

I found one of the biggest benefits was opening up—not just physically through the meridians, but spiritually as well. Luke talked a lot about Lao Tzu and the *Tao Te Ching*. He has spent 8 years translating it into Chinese and English and finding new layers. He kept referring to long life Tao. It seems the essence is love yourself, love others, and love the environment—no hate or violence. Not a bad philosophy. Fortunately, the teaching was almost entirely consistent with Gurdjieff, so I didn't have to get caught up in intellectual games. He did talk about fate, but his point of view was that we need to accept whatever happens, go with the flow of it, and stay open to new possibilities. It doesn't suggest determinism or things happening for a reason. It's more aligned with finding your own reason and creating meaning out of whatever happens. There is no need to carry baggage. Life is.

In the mornings, we went to Luke's mother-in-law's apartment for our morning practice. I called her Mama Chi. We did over an hour of lift chi up, pull chi down. One day, at the end of the practice we were all chatting up a storm like typical Westerners and Mama Chi stopped us and said, "Quiet . . . . Inside . . . . Chi." It was her kind way of saying shut the fuck up and stay with your Chi.

In one of the Tao sessions, I had an insight.

	Body	Mind	Spirit
Intention			
Conductor			
Sensation			

Intention is in the head and sets goals. Conductor is the chi ball in our abdomen. Sensation is conscious awareness. The Tao is the wholeness of body, mind, and spirit. It's the harmony of One. My insight was that you can apply intention, conductor, and sensation to body, mind and spirit. For me, I have fairly good intentions about the care of my body, mind, and spirit, but my conductor doesn't know how to orchestrate the energy to accomplish any real goals, and I was not experiencing any sensations that would enable me to measure progress on those goals.

Luke talked fairly extensively about the history and philosophy of Tao and the lineage of Chi Lel Qi Gong. He kept emphasizing that Lao Tzu wrote the *Tao Te Ching* 2,600 years ago and the principles still hold true. He mentioned that Stephen Hawking uses similar language to describe why the *Tao Te Ching* is a vital text, for example describing the two basic human genes as aggressiveness and desire. Gurdjieff uses the terms ego and desire to describe the same phenomenon. Luke kept referring to the idea that we are holograms trying to connect with a super hologram i.e. from the center everything is One.

Luke also reinforced my bias that gurus and religions often manipulate people for purposes of power and control, the same theme that Nietzsche expounded upon. He shared his personal history of building a large following and lecturing around the world on Chi Lel Qi Gong and then deciding to come back to his roots when he started to get caught up in the whole "money business." He cited several examples of gurus thinking they are above the rules, keeping secrets to themselves to maintain their edge, and then using their exalted status to exploit people either financially or sexually.

There is no question that Luke is an extraordinary master, and yet he has very little ego and desire. His primary focus is to finish his translation/interpretation of the *Tao Te Ching* and to help others develop qigong skills. It's mind boggling that a person with his capabilities is charging $100 per day for food, lodging, and life-changing training—not withholding any "secrets" and acting with complete humility. He talked about the Tao belief that the universe was created out of nothing, a perspective that Stephen Hawking also wrote about in the *Brief History of Time.* The basic point is that before Nothingness, there was the Nameless

What became clear in the training was that one key to developing healing energy is the Psoas muscle below the diaphragm that can control our breathing. Luke kept emphasizing that we were all born as Grand Masters. All you have to do is watch a baby breathe to see that they breathe from their diaphragm and that their back muscles expand and contract. We lose that ability as we get older and as we move away from our core and into our heads. As a result, this muscle has atrophied. One purpose of the training is to re-discover and rebuild that muscle. The muscle alone won't help us connect with a higher energy, but without a fully developed Psoas, it's impossible to move from intention to sensation, to generate healing energy, to get in harmony with the rhythm of the universe, or to develop a powerful presence. All of Luke's joints move as if they were circular pulleys.

One morning we discussed the core values of Taoism: simplicity, decency, and cosmic connection. From my work in culture change, I know that the best path to creating organizational soul is to focus on a few key values. It seems to me that the world could benefit if everyone mobilized around these core values. Indeed, it may be our only hope to save the planet from our genetic instincts of aggression and desire and our never-ending propensity for hate and violence.

One particular exercise we practiced during the retreat was to imagine an elephant trunk extending from the coccyx and to use our hips to create a circle on the ground between our feet. With every circle, there is a release and absorb portion with a "stop" in between for relaxation and cosmic connection. I felt my whole lower back open up and relax—all the tension was gone. As a result, I have been able to walk more freely than I have in a long time.

Just when I was thinking I was getting more proficient with my "conductor," Luke introduced the techniques for increasing sensation. The instructions on "release" were to start with the shoulder blade and then move to the shoulder, the elbow, the wrist, and the three sets of joints on the hand; and on "absorb" to reverse the process. The goal was to increase the sensation at each point while imagining the shoulder, elbow, wrist, and three sets of hand joints as circles with no tension. We were told to focus on all these points as we continued to "turn" with our conductor. It's an incredibly challenging mental and physical challenge. I can see why qigong helps to improve memory—it's a real work-out for the brain. I told Luke that this training is like boot camp for marines because it is so rigorous and challenging. The only difference is that he is producing peace machines instead of killing machines.

I discovered that by incorporating "release" and "absorb" into my meditation there is a noticeable new quality. I experienced a more natural rhythm, I was able to experience finer sensations, and the words seemed to have new meaning given our Tao discussions and qigong exercises.

Reflecting on the whole training experience, I am amazed at how well orchestrated each day was. We went to Mama Chi's apartment for an hour of gigong and breakfast—usually noodles, soup, and fruit. We returned to our apartment after breakfast and worked with Luke until 12:30. We then went upstairs to Luke's apartment and had lunch. We took a break from 1-3, so I would go for a long walk outside the compound and take a nap. We worked again from 3-6:30 and went back upstairs for dinner—a variety of several delicious vegetable options with one selection of poultry or fish. The food was nutritious, tasty and healthy—no wine, no chocolate, no red meat, and no dairy. We returned to our apartment at 7:30 and either walked a block down the street for a massage at the spa (open 7 days a week until midnight) or did another practice session with Mama Chi in her apartment.

Luke's daily training sessions were also very well designed. Each new technique was tell, show, do. Luke usually began with a colorful and impassioned commentary on Tao that gave us perspective and context. Then he explained the skill we would learn and demonstrated how to do it. Unlike most masters, he let us feel how his muscles turned and he shared openly the secrets he has learned. He had no desire to be held up on a pedestal or to be revered as a guru. He kept reinforcing the point that we are our own masters. We just need to rediscover the gifts we had when we were babies and have lost through ego, desire, and cultural seduction.

Luke talked frequently about how egos can get in the way of Tao. His point was that when you say you've got it, you have lost it. He had a wonderful way of telling stories and jokes to make teaching points. In this case, he was making the point that the training is more than techniques, it's about who we are as human beings on this earth.

Over the course of the training, I realized how much tension I carry in my body. Qigong is designed to help us move more effortlessly and to stay calm and centered in the midst of any storm. In essence, it is the science of movement. The practice of release and absorb helps to identify the tension points and let them go.

As the training progressed I made significant progress on increasing sensation. In addition to releasing, absorbing, and turning, we learned to fine-tune our sensation. During each release and absorb, we focused on seven points from our shoulder blades to the tips of our fingers (between the shoulder blades, shoulder, elbow, wrist, big knuckles, middle knuckles, and finger-tip knuckles). By the end of the training, I was able to feel the sensation moving up and down my arms from the tips of my fingers to the middle of my shoulder blades. It required a great deal of concentration because I had to do four things at once: practice the form, release and absorb, turn the imaginary chi ball in my abdomen by using the psoas muscle, and feel the sensations along seven points on my arms. In those few moments when I was able to accomplish all four tasks at once, it put me in a trance-like state.

Luke's Tao lessons were always inspiring and thought provoking. I realized how Tao and qigong can enhance every aspect of life. Luke described how important it is to act as a mirror and to reflect what another person is saying without being judgmental. Instead of arguing who is right and wrong, the idea is to let go of that argument and accept that, in the larger scheme of things, it doesn't really matter. Assuming that attitude doesn't absolve you from taking a stand to protect yourself, others, and the environment. Using our model of Get-Give-Merge-Go, it is possible to get the other person's perspective in a non-judgmental way, give my perspective in a gentle way, merge points of common agreement, and agree on actions that serve everyone's best interest, i.e. build grow-grow relationships.

I also learned a great deal about Taoism, Buddhism, and Confucianism. Apparently, much of Buddhism is derived from Taoism. Both are more internally focused. Confucianism, on the other hand, emphasizes external control with the emperor having the last word in all matters.

Given my obsession with scales, I built on the previous discussion and created a new scale for spiritual evolution.

5.0: Being
4.0: Seeing
3.0: Doing
2.0: Knowing
1.0: Ignoring or Emptying

Ignoring is a negative state in which we engage in willful stupidity. We don't want to learn or grow, and we don't listen to any other perspective beyond our own rigid, ideological dogma. Emptying, however, can be a positive state that enables us to let go of ego and desire and to begin each moment as a baby: open, curious, and connected to the cosmos. It is the realization that we are nothing.

Knowing means that we are actively inquiring about our worlds and trying to learn as much as we can about the meaning of life and who we are. Knowledge results from the efforts we make to create our own theology or philosophy. It requires disciplined, rigorous intellectual effort.

Doing means that we are mindful of our behaviors and seek to act in ways that are congruent with our knowledge and beliefs. Like knowing, this stage of development is still externally oriented, but it requires great physical, emotional and intellectual effort to close the gap between what we know and what we do.

Seeing means that we are able to observe with impartial objectivity our lower self and our higher self. It means that we have conscious awareness of the gap between who we are and who we want to become. Seeing requires that we stay in front of the gap between our ideal self and our ordinary self and that we suffer intentionally from living in that gap. We feel organic shame that we aren't doing more to help others, the earth, and God. At the same time, we see that our ego doesn't really matter. At level 4, there is a strong connection with our higher energy. This marks the shift from external to internal.

Being means that we are at One with the Universe and with everything and everyone in it. This state of being may occur fleetingly in a moment of enlightenment and then pass as we return to our habits and daydreaming. We need to return to, as Luke would say, "Baby," in which state we are again empty so that we can recycle the process at a different and deeper layer. Those moments of being, however, increase our presence, our power, and our ability to have an impact on ourselves, others, and our environment.

As I got more proficient at the skills of turning and sensing, I was able to experience deeper states of consciousness. It became easier to turn, release, absorb, sense, and practice the form all at the same time. I realized, however, that there is a huge gap between what is possible and where I am. Those fleeting moments, when I was in the rhythm and harmonized with chi, felt freeing.

One particularly challenging Tao lesson had to do with getting in rhythm with the pulse of the universe. Evidently, physicists have found that the pulse is getting faster which may account for the increasing madness in the world.

One goal I created during the training was to develop an engine to power the forms. My engine is only about 2 horsepower at this point but I hope to keep adding power as I continue to practice. Doing the forms without the engine is like putting a lawn mower engine into a Porsche. It may look good, but it won't do much. It's what's inside that counts and whether or not I am connected to a higher energy. If I can become One with the Universe, it is possible to form a "Real I" and to have a unique impact on others and on the environment. There is a huge gap between where I am now and that state.

Luke talked a lot about the importance of simplicity. He said the world belongs to everyone, and we need to become One with it. It's more important to share than to accumulate. And why bother. We don't even possess our bodies. How can we think we can possess anything else? And why should we want to? A bird only needs a branch to live in the forest. I only need one breath to live in the next moment.

He continually stressed the importance of staying quiet inside and finding new responses to changing conditions. In the moment of crisis, let go of techniques and just be there. After all, he said, great sports performances come when you are not thinking about it. Champions seem to somehow tap into higher energies.

The immersion in the Chinese culture helped immeasurably. Also, I found that the intensity and duration of the training were completely necessary. I learned experientially that the way to raise energy is to drop tension. Every move we make entails dropping sensation from the shoulder blades to the finger tips. What makes a difference is increasing conscious awareness of all the tension points along the way—7 to be exact.

What I appreciate about qigong is that it is not guru-centric. Everyone is his or her own master. Qigong has transferred the Tai Chi principles of fighting into healing.

As the training progressed, my conductor started working more smoothly and effortlessly and my sensors became more finely tuned. I started visualizing my body as a straight line with balancing bowls on each side. That image enabled me to feel much more relaxed and keep my shoulders dropped. It's shocking to me how much tension I had been carrying around, but I started to move more slowly, loosely, and relaxed.

Since I have talked so much about Luke, I thought a brief sketch of his life might be helpful. He was born and raised in Zhong Shan. In 1966, at age 14, he and his family managed to get on the last train out of China before Mao closed the borders and initiated the Cultural Revolution. Luke lived in Hong Kong for 9 years where he started his Tai Chi training and went to school. When he was 23, he moved to the US and lived there for 25 years. He started out in Texas (where he went to college), moved to Florida, and conducted workshops across the US and Europe. In 2000, Luke returned to China where he continues to live and work. He has been married and divorced. His second marriage was to a woman who is 20 years younger than he is. He had a baby boy, Peter, with her. Peter is now 10 years old. Luke is totally devoted to him.

Every day of the training brought delightful surprises and new challenges. One morning we did an exercise sitting down and moved our shoulders as we absorbed chi. I felt like a bird. That afternoon we did a ball exercise, and I felt like a total klutz. Sometimes the exercises seemed so natural and effortless and at other times they felt completely impossible. Of course, Luke made them all look easy.

One day, Luke discussed the influence of the *I Ching* on the *Tao Te Ching*, Taoism, Buddhism, and Confucianism. The *I Ching* is known as the book of changes and has been used historically by people to predict the future. Luke prefers to see it as a book of wisdom that facilitates reflection. As has happened with many great ideas, the *I Ching* was hijacked by Confucianism to reinforce a hierarchical governing structure and the ultimate authority of the Emperor. Luke believes that the primary messages of the *Tao Te Ching* are 1) we are One and 2) our purpose in life is to love others, love ourselves, and love the environment.

Taoism is based on the theory that out of the Nameless Nothing comes One, out of One comes heaven and earth, and out of heaven and earth came the first cellular organisms that have evolved into the multitudinous life forms we have today. What's important is to see all life in connection with the Whole, not just as separate. We also need to see that emptiness is required for fullness to occur. Luke presented all these ideas in a passionate and transparent way. He listened to our questions and did not try to impose his points of view.

Toward the end of the training, Luke discussed his eight years of work to translate and interpret the *Tao Te Ching*. He emphasized the importance of translating from the original text first and then making interpretations. He is committed to doing a rigorous substantiation of each original and then applying an organizing construct to identify themes. The primary principles are simplicity, interdependence, and humility. According to the *Tao Te Ching*, Tao is unexhausted and un-exhaustable. It is all about giving instead of getting. Luke emphasized that one theme in the *Tao Te Ching* is that we breathe as the universe breathes and that nothing belongs to us. Since the Tao gives unselfishly, what gives us the right to be selfish? We need to be at One instead of separate, and yet life continually sucks us into separateness. The goal is integration, not isolation. We are Nothing and Everything at the same time.

For Luke, long life Tao is the anchor and motivates love vs. fear. He believes we are born Grand Masters instead of sinners—another point of view I liked. Long life Tao is a combination of love + effort. It takes a lot of effort to reach an effortless state.

The training not only enhanced my practice, but also enriched my understanding of philosophy. Here's a great quote from verse #70 of the *Tao Te Ching*: "To know and yet think we do not know is the highest attainment; not to know and yet think we do know is a disease."

Luke talked about 3 levels of living:

Level 1: Constantly reacting from the lower self with no conscious awareness of the experience. The lower self is very active and the higher self is practically absent.

Level 2: Noticing the interaction of the lower and higher selves with the higher self being more active and lower self being more passive. Being able to experience some connection with higher energy.

Level 3: Feeling at One with the Universe and having only one judgment: Long Life Tao: Love myself, love others, love the environment.

Getting to level 2 requires mental, physical, emotional spiritual effort. Getting to level 3 requires removing the mind as an obstacle, effortlessly connecting with higher energy, and feeling at One with the Universe.

While staying at level 3 is reserved for saints and gurus, it is possible to expand the moments of oneness before returning to our ordinary lives at level 1 or 2. My belief is that experiencing and expanding level 3 moments will help me get more quickly out of level 1 life and will help me increase my conscious awareness in level 2. Through years of effort and practice, I hope to experience more level 3 moments.

What struck me is that 2600 years ago, the *Tao Te Ching* laid out the primary principles for sustainable development on our earth. In verse #31, it states flat out that weapons are evil. If you don't have to use them, you shouldn't. If you do have to use them, you should avoid glorifying your victories and you should grieve the losses of your enemies as well as your own. I guess we haven't learned that lesson very well.

In verse #30, The Tao says not to use military force to conquer, because you can't conquer minds through force. If you do have to use force, then you should stop when you achieve pre-determined results. The goal should not be to conquer. If you are able to achieve your objectives, then there should be no bragging or arrogance. The most important principle is to use military force with great reluctance and as a last resort. Hmmm, another lesson unlearned.

What puzzles me is that if we have known these principles for 2600 years, why have we continually failed to act on them? Verse #70 has a reason. In that verse, the Tao says that words are easy to understand, but they are hard to put into practice. Those who understand are few and those who emulate the principles are rare.

The real question is how do we break out of this cycle of violence and hatred. Based on many discussions during the training, I would say there are three steps:

1. Embrace the idea of Oneness. If we see that we are all One, then we may be reluctant to kill each other. We need to focus on developing people instead of controlling them.
2. Understand that pain drives a lot of behavior and that we all have our private pain we are dealing with.
3. Practice forgiveness and compassion given your belief in 1 and 2 above.

If a critical mass of people would take those steps seriously, we might have a chance of saving ourselves and saving the earth. Again, being achieves more than doing.

Luke differentiated Buddhist's beliefs in the next life to Taoist beliefs. Buddhists believe there are endless reincarnations and that your karma follows you into each life. Taoism believes that we are born enlightened beings and we need to return to that state. Taoists believe in immortality independent of our actions in each life. Feels a little like magical thinking to me.

Luke shared with us the eight principles that he has derived from his translation of the *Tao Te Ching*. I took the liberty to put my own spin on his words and expanded the list to 16. Here are the principles I heard:

1. Love each other.
   - No hate
2. Love interdependence. We are One. Everything is related.
   - No separation
3. Greet each day with gratitude.
   - No complaining
4. Share what you have. Enough is enough. The world is for everyone.
   - No accumulation
5. Love peace.
   - No war
   - No religion
   - No country
6. Live life fully.
   - No negativity
   - No superficiality
   - No pretending
7. Silently keep the center.
   - No noise
8. Connect with the cosmos.
   - No mental interference
9. Seize the moment. Act now.
   - No procrastination
   - No laziness
10. Make effort.
    - No waiting for things to happen without work
    - No wishing
    - No imagination

11. Trust in the universe. Find the gift in the good and the bad.
    - No victimhood
12. Return to the enlightened being of your infancy.
    - No blame
13. Anticipate and prepare.
    - No excuses
14. Stand up for yourself, others, and the environment.
    - No fear.
    - No cowardice.
15. Laugh at success and failure.
    - No attachment
    - No pride
    - No identification
    - No exaggeration
16. Grow perspective.
    - No delusion

These principles all make terrific sense to me. As guidelines and aspirations, they are as meaningful as any set I've ever heard.

Chapter #51 in the Tao says that virtue is valued. Again, I don't know. The final point Luke made is that people become evil when their mind is blocked from the light. That blockage could come from a combination of circumstances beyond their control or from their own choices. Accepting that possibility eases the path to forgiveness.

At times we digressed into a discussion of Chinese history and current political and educational policy. The point that came out of the discussion was that it doesn't work to go to extremes on any particular theory. I summarized the generic points by saying, it's rarely either/or. In education, it's not memorize or process; it's both. In government or parenting, its not freedom or control; it's both. In learning, it's not acquire or apply; it's both. As human beings, it's not respond or initiate; it's both.

This conversation gave me a better understanding of my experience with qigong. I had acquired the techniques and skills, but I couldn't apply them to every movement as I went through each day. And for the last 15 years of practicing the qigong form, I had applied the form, but I hadn't acquired the skills that gave power to the form. I was just going through the motions.

Luke said that the emphasis in Chinese education has shifted from rote memorization with no processing to processing with no memorization. Both are mistakes. What the Chinese government is struggling with is how to balance control and freedom. These "either/ors" are at the core of many issues. If we are going to get out of the mess we are in, we need to:

Memorize AND Process
Free AND Control
Acquire AND Apply
Respond AND Initiate.

In one afternoon session, Luke said the purpose of qigong is readiness for life: calm and centered in every moment for every circumstance. An encouraging idea is that if you tell a cell what to do, it behaves. We have 50 trillion cells in our body, but one cell can make a difference on the whole bunch.

In another session, we had a frustrating conversation about the scientific underpinnings of qigong. Luke was trying to explain how natural forces relate to gigong practices. The four forces are gravity, weak nuclear, strong nuclear, and electromagnetism. Gravity is for grounding. The nuclear forces are related to turning and electro-magnetic radiation is related to energy. I liked the idea of looking at the science of spirituality, but it was confusing. What did come out of the discussion as useful was the idea that "turning" is based on the same principles as star dust and the turning of the planets around the sun. I also liked the ideas that we are held by space/time in our movements and that we are trying to get our bodies to work like pulleys—mind over muscle.

I did some research to try to get a better understanding of what Luke had been talking about relative to the Jing Qi Shen and natural forces. Now I know why I was confused. The Jing Qi Shen is known as the three treasures in China or the essential energies for sustaining life. Jing is defined as vital essence, spirit, libido, sperm, or sexual energy. Qi is defined as energy, vitality, force, breath, and spirit. Shen is defined as spirit, soul, mind, or deity. As you can see, there is no clear definition of any of the three and there are overlapping definitions, e.g. spirit is used to define all three.

Digging deeper I found that Shen leads the Qi which leads the Jing. Or, in another slant, Jing is transformed into Chi which can be transformed into Shen, i.e. sexual energy can be transformed into vital energy, which can be transformed into spiritual energy or soul. It's all very confusing, but at least I deepened my understanding of what he was talking about.

Toward the end of the training, Luke answered the big question of how to reach a state of effortless effort: to be held by space/time, to generate energy by turning, and by deepening sensation by seeing the body joints as pulleys.

Luke ended three weeks of training, with some particularly profound statements:

- The music and sounds of humans and earth come from the silence of the universe.
- According to chaos theory, the smallest change in initial conditions can yield dramatically different results. Lorenz, a MIT mathematician, called this the butterfly effect, i.e. a flap of a butterfly in Brazil can cause a tornado in Texas. Applying this theory to health means that we can create small cellular changes by tapping into higher energy to yield equally dramatic health outcomes.
- Life and death are not separate.
- Qigong is simply learning methods to return to our Grand Master state as babies. We are already "there," we just forgot it.
- He who says "I have no ego" has the biggest ego.

Luke was a delight to listen to. He was passionate, transparent, and generous. And he had no need or desire to be treated like a Guru. He occasionally got so excited about his ideas that he would ramble on, but it was worth it to stick with him because he was always dropping pearls of wisdom and helpful observations.

So, that concludes an overview of one small step I took in an attempt to stimulate a giant leap for all of us. I hope the road markers on my path trigger ideas for you to pursue your own path.

COMING HOME

I retuned from China to many homes. I returned to America—a land I love. I came back to my family—the people I love most in the world. I came back to my physical environment that I treasure. And yes, I came back a little more in touch with my internal HOME. As Luke said, "We simply need to come back to our own HOME of unconditional love. We are all enlightened beings even though we may forget our inner baby inside."

When I meditate and do qigong now, I try to connect with the Light, Warmth, and Love in the Universe. I imagine opening up to the stars, the Milky Way, the Universe, and to Infinity and try to bring all that positive energy into my body. Somehow the path from the universe to our inner HOME is littered with the debris of our cultural conditioning and personal experiences. Yet, when I look into the eyes of my baby grandchildren, I see unfiltered Light, Warmth, and Love. It's already there. And I wonder. What will happen to bring a shadow to that Light, to put a chill in that warmth, to turn that love into hate? What happens in peoples' lives that transform them from innocent and pure babies to dark, cold, and bitter adults? My observation is that they wander away from their HOME and their center in search of a different home away from themselves. Why is returning to the HOME that is already there fraught with so many obstacles?

The road from essence to personality is so much easier than the road from personality to essence. The road from substance to appearance is far more seductive than the road from appearance to substance. But that's another book.

I also have returned to a spiritual home—All Souls Unitarian Universalist Community in Manhattan. The following hymn is one of the reasons I feel so at home in this community. It's Hymn #158 in the UU Hymnal.

> *"Praise the source of faith and learning that has sparked and stoked the mind*
> *with a passion for discerning how the world has been designed.*
> *Let the sense of wonder flowing from the wonders we survey*
> *keep our faith forever growing and renew our need to pray.*
> *Source of wisdom, we acknowledge that our science and our art*
> *and the breadth of human knowledge only partial truth impart.*
> *Far beyond our calculation lies a depth we cannot sound*
> *where the purpose for creation and the pulse of life are found.*
> *May our faith redeem the blunder of believing that our thought*
> *has displaced the grounds for wonder which the ancient prophets taught.*

> *May our learning curb the error which unthinking faith*
> *   can breed*
> *lest we justify some terror with an antiquated creed.*
> *Praise for minds to probe the heavens, praise for strength*
> *   to breathe the air,*
> *praise for all that beauty leavens, praise for silence,*
> *   music, prayer.*
> *Praise for justice and compassion and for strangers,*
> *   neighbors, friends,*
> *praise for hearts and lips to fashion, praise for love that*
> *   never ends."*

The UU hymn and the following Rumi poem capture the essence of this book.

Whoever Brought Me Here, Will Have To Take Me Home

> *"All day I think about it, then at night I say it. Where did I come from, and what am I supposed to be doing? I have no idea. My soul is from elsewhere, I'm sure of that, and I intend to end up there.*
>
> *This drunkenness began in some other tavern. When I get back around to that place, I'll be completely sober. Meanwhile, I'm like a bird from another continent, sitting in this aviary. The day is coming when I fly off, but who is it now in my ear who hears my voice? Who says words with my mouth?*
>
> *Who looks out with my eyes? What is the soul? I cannot stop asking. If I could taste one sip of an answer, I could break out of this prison for drunks. I didn't come here of my*

own accord, and I can't leave that way. Whoever brought me here, will have to take me HOME.

This poetry. I never know what I'm going to say. I don't plan it. When I'm outside the saying of it, I get very quiet and rarely speak at all"

Rumi raises the critical challenge, "if I could get a sip of an answer, I could break out of this prison for drunks." This book simply describes my search for that elusive sip. It seems to me that the only way out is to go deep inside and work through. Only by great effort will be able to find our HOME.

Independent of whatever the end may be, I can't think of a more fulfilling process. As we try to find a way out of this prison for drunks, the idea is to increase the moments of peace, possibility, and connection in our lives. We need to realize there are always going to be intruders in our home. Accept them. Laugh at them. Come from a place of peace, possibility, and connection. That's all we can do on a personal level.

On a global level, Nationhood may be a necessary step along the way. The only real solution for lasting peace on our planet, however, is for people to build internal HOMES—connected to the universe and to a nameless force and source. To bask in gratitude that we are here now—an impossible probability now manifest in amazing possibility. And figure out a way to get along peacefully and collaboratively.

There are some major challenges to achieve that goal. In my view, we need to let go of identification, imagination, and negative emotion. We need to create a crystalized "I" with no need for power, fame, or control.

Roger Cohen, the New York Times columnist, says it more simply:

> "Somewhere deep inside everyone is the thing that makes them tick. The thing is it is often well hidden. The psyche builds layers of protection around people's most vulnerable traits, which may be closely linked to their precious essence. Social media build layers of distraction from that essence."

Building a HOME requires silence and reflection. Two states that are hard to achieve in this noisy world. Twitter, e-mail, etc. reinforce skimming. Building a HOME means going deep.

So, be quiet
Be still
Be calm
Be at peace
Return to your true HOME

Our unruly I's will always raise their ugly heads. They are like snakes in the path of a horse. We lose all control. What's important is to stay committed to a continuing process and keep the faith that evolution and growth are possible.

On a personal note, my journey continues. I have learned to use my Tourette symptoms as early warning signs of stress and to quickly employ my qigong skills to release tension and find a state of equanimity. As soon as I observe myself emitting involuntary tics, I go to my center. This process quickly releases the tension and the tics. And my qi gong/meditation practice has increased from 15 minutes to an hour. As I go slower, I get better.

Also, I re-connected with an old friend from Vietnam, Artie Egendorf, who is now a Pranic Healer and a Feldencrais practitioner. After graduating from Harvard and completing a doctorate in Clinical Pyschology from Yeshiva, Artie has been on a parallel path to mine. He has now formed a new company, Super Integral Synergy, which helps people power-charge their healing process and bring boundless blessings to themselves and others. By teaching me some simple techniques, he has made it possible for me to prolong and deepen my states of consciousness and awareness.

With Artie's methodology, you move from making deliberate movements, to allowing yourself to be moved, to experiencing a boundless grace. At first, it is necessary to learn the forms and practice the moves. That step requires deliberate consciousness. Then, as you get into the rhythm and flow of the movements, you allow yourself to be moved and to experience a Oneness and Harmony. It is the transition from "doing" to "being." Finally, as you let go to the rhythm, you let in the love of the Universe and feel the abundant blessings of Being. The movements become a dance that enables you to glide through life like a river over rocks. And you learn to transform every step and every movement into a dance.

As I mentioned in the beginning of the book, the goal is to achieve more Near Life Experiences while we exist on earth. The dancing represents a transition from a Near Life Experience to a Full Life experience—at least for a moment.

The key to all of this is cycle time. How long does it take to find my way HOME after I get pulled out, sucked out, or drawn out of it. As my journey continues, I hope to reduce that cycle time, increase my energy, and improve the quality of my life and others.

Moving forward together, we need to find a community for our HOMES. A sense of connection is essential. Even though we try to power our individual homes with universal light, love, and warmth, we need to create a connected community as well in order to have a greater impact on this earth and to save the planet from climate change and nuclear disaster.

In his book, *The Empathic Civilization*, Jeremy Rifkin discusses how civilization, over the past 3,000 years, has moved from a mythological consciousness, to a theological consciousness, to an ideological consciousness, to a psychological consciousness, and finally to a biosphere consciousness. He suggests that we have evolved emotionally as well as physically. If true, this is a hopeful trend. We will need to evolve emotionally and spiritually if we are going to save our planet. If we could distribute the percentage of people in the world over the past 3,000 years who function primarily with one of these states of consciousness, we would find that a shift is occurring. I would hypothesize that few people still have a mythological consciousness and there seems to be a decreasing percentage of people who have a theological consciousness. Clearly, we live in an age in which ideological and psychological consciousness are more predominant. Unfortunately, a very small percentage of the world has a biosphere consciousness—the critical requirement for saving the planet. The only question is can we make the shift as a civilization to a biosphere consciousness quickly enough to avoid disaster.

In conclusion, I believe that we need to find a HOME that gives us a sense of peace and a foundation for being more loving and responsible. I wrote this poem to summarize my point of view.

> This HOME is not a fortress to protect your personality
> It is a place that frees your essence.

> This HOME is not a building to defend your thoughts
>> and beliefs
> It is an inner warmth that has no fence.
> This HOME is not an external place to give you a sense
>> of order.
> It is an internal launching pad to release your energy
>> beyond any border.
> This HOME is not a retreat to make you feel selected.
> It is a simple sensibility that enables you to feel connected.

At a minimum, consciousness and awareness are good things independent of any transcendent possibilities. Being conscious means we have a capable CEO overseeing our zombie operating systems. Being aware means we have few blind spots, some level of sensitivity to others, and a feeling of being alive and awake for our brief period on this earth. At a maximum, being conscious means we develop a crystalized essence; a connection to higher energies; a Oneness with the Absolute; a higher probability for another chance; an enlightened state; an evolutionary advance; an ultimate liberation from the trials of this world; a greater appreciation for what's unfolding in front of us, a feeling of freedom from our habits, limitations, and constricting beliefs; a deeper and richer understanding of possibility; a sense of unification; and a more powerful ability to heal with the light, love, and warmth of the universe. On a collective level, it creates the energy required to develop a biosphere consciousness and to save the earth from ourselves.

And death becomes just another moment.

May you find your HOME and be at peace. May we find a way to dance all the way to death. And, together, may we find a way to join with each other as one community on earth dedicated to the preservation of the planet and to the generation of new possibilities for all.

I can't think of a better way to end this book, than sharing some lyrics of one of my favorite songs by Leonard Cohen, *Dance Me to the End of Love*. If there is anyone who is at HOME in the Universe, it is this wonderful songwriter and poet.

Dance me to your beauty with a burning violin
Dance me through the panic 'til I'm gathered safely in
Lift me like an olive branch and be my homeward dove
Dance me to the end of love

REFERENCES

Barks, C. The Essential Rumi. Harper Collins, 1996.

Bynner, Witter. The Way of Life: According to Laotzu. Berkley Publishing, 1986.

Carkhuff, R. R. Human Possibilities. Amherst, MA: HRD Press, 2000.

Carkhuff, R. R. The Age of Ideation. HRD Press, 2007.

Chbosky, S. The Perks of Being a Wallflower. Simon and Schuster, 1999.

DeSalzmann, Jeanne. The Reality of Being: the fourth way of Gurdjieff. Shambhala, 2010.

DeYoung, C. G., Hirsch, J.B., Shane, M. S., Papademetris, X., Rajeevan, N., & Gray, J. R. (2010). Testing predictions from personality neuroscience: Brain structure and the Big Five. Psychological Science, 21, 820-828.

Diamond, Jared. Guns, Germs, and Steel, Norton, 1997.

Eagleman, David. Incognito: the secret lives of the brain. Pantheon, 2011.

Eben, Alexander. Proof of Heaven: A neurosurgeon's journey into the afterlife. Simon and Shuster, 2012.

Ellis, Albert. Rational Emotive Behavior Therapy. APA, 2011.

Gurdjieff, G. I. In Search of Being: the fourth way to consciousness. Shambhala, 2012.

Gurdfieff, G. I. Beelzebub's Tales to his Grandson: All and Everything. Penguin, 1950.

Hawking, Stephen. A Brief History of Time. Bantam, 1988.

Kahneman, Daniel. Thinking Fast and Slow. New York. Farrar, Straus and Giroux, 2011.

Koch, Christof. Consciousness: confessions of a romantic reductionist. MIT Press, 2012.

Nietzsche, F. Beyond Good and Evil. Tribeca Books, 1910.

Reich, Wilhelm. Character Analysis. Farrar, Straus, Giroux, 1945.

Rifkin, Jeremy. The Empathic Civilization: the race to global consciousness in a world in crisis. Penguin, 2009.

ABOUT THE AUTHOR

Richard (Rick) Bellingham has over 30 years of experience as an organizational psychologist in executive coaching, strategic planning, organizational learning, and leadership development. He has consulted with over 200 organizations worldwide at the C-suite level. Rick has worked with executives in over half of the Fortune 100 companies during the course of his career. He has extensive experience coaching in high tech, telecommunications, health care, financial, and professional service firms.

Rick is the CEO of iobility (www.iobility.com), a New York based consulting group, and has been an adjunct faculty member at Harvard University, where he co-founded the Forum for Intelligent Organizations, as well as Duke and Cornell. In addition, he has taught culture change, healthcare management, and leadership development at several universities.

Rick has held executive positions within corporate settings including SVP of Human Resources at Parametric Technology, VP of Organizational Learning at Genzyme, and Director of

Health Promotion, Samaritan Health Service. Additionally, he has provided pro-bono services at the Board level for the past 25 years for organizations including the YMCA, Visiting Nurses Association, and Homeless Solutions.

As a consultant, Rick has provided executive coaching feedback, training, and leadership development in companies ranging from small businesses to large multi-nationals. Rick has worked extensively in Asia, Europe and Latin America. He has published numerous articles in peer-reviewed publications and has written 15 books on parenting, wellness, leadership, culture, and HR strategy.

His books include *The Fables of Boris: Raising Healthy Children, Creating Organizational Soul, Spiritual Leadership, The Complete Guide to Wellness, Designing Effective Health Promotion Programs, The Culture Change Sourcebook, The Wellness Sourcebook, Leadership Lexicon, Ethical Leadership, Leadership Myths and Realities, Getting People and Culture Right in Mergers and Acquisitions, HR Optimization, Corporate Culture Change, Virtual Teams,* and *Intellectual Capital Development.*

Rick holds an Ed.D. in Counseling Psychology. He has been married for 43 years, has two children, Rebecca and Emily, and two grandchildren, Annie and Ezra. He and his wife, Bobbitt, split their time between Brooklyn, NY and Traverse City, Michigan.